Good Music is Better Than Sex

To order additional copies, please contact us.
BookSurge, LLC
www.booksurge.com
1-866-308-6235
orders@booksurge.com

JUDY CORE

Good Music Is Better Than Sex

My Search For The Old Blue Chair

2006

Good Music is Better Than Sex

ACKNOWLEDGEMENTS

Old Blue Chair ©2004 Sony/ATV Tunes, LLC, Islandsoul Music. All rights administered by Sony/ATV Music Publishing 8 Music Square West, Nashville, TN 37203. All rights reserved. Used by permission.

Dreams ©2002 Sony/ATV Songs, LLC Roots and Boots Music, Write On Music. All rights on behalf of Sony/ATV Songs LLC, Roots and Boots Music administered by Sony/ATV Music Publishing, 8 Music Square West, Nashville, TN 37203. Used by permission.

The Stages of Committed Relationships

http://www.relationship-institute.com/freearticles_detail.cfm?article_ID=153

I'd like to send a special thank you to the following: all the folks at BookSurge, Rebecca, my wonderful editor, Judy Stevens-Long, my mentor, and everyone in my life that has supported this endeavor. Kenny Chesney sums it up best for me in his song "Old Bird Dog", "I thank God for the life He lets me have".

***

This Book Is Dedicated To A Man Who Has Absolutely No Idea I Exist. However Unknowingly, He Still Has Had The Most Amazing Impact On My Life.
Kenny Chesney, Your Music Released An Artistic, Creative Side Of Myself That Was Buried For As Long As I Can Remember. I Thank You For Sharing Your Gift With The World. You Have An Amazing Talent For Connecting To Others. Thank You For Putting Yourself Out There Artistically As A Songwriter And For Taking The Risk Of Be As You Are (Songs From An Old Blue Chair).
Lastly, Thank You For The Blue Chair, For Helping Me To Be As I Am, And For Giving Me The Magic Of This Island.

JMC
December 5, 2005 3:03 Am
32 Catherineberg
St. John, USVI

FORWARD
The Voice of Music

Kenny Chesney has won several top honors and awards in the country music industry. However, there is one that I personally believe holds the most weight, the most credibility, and of which he is the most deserving. It also aptly describes his gift and his talent.

The ASCAP award, entitled the "Voice of Music Award," is given to "Songwriters whose music gives people's lives a voice through song." Only four others have received this honor—Garth Brooks, Amy Grant, Diane Warren and George Strait. Kenny Chesney was awarded this honor October 17, 2005.

This book is about the voice of music. The voice of lyrics. The power of words. I am speaking of the skilled ability of one person to take his emotions, feelings and other indescribable social constructs and then translate them into words, song and music, which then has the power to connect with someone miles away. It is not linear. It is a fluid process.

The one with the gift can speak and be the voice for those like me. I am one who struggles to put my emotions and feelings into a meaningful descriptive sentence, never mind being able to complete a package of words, musical notes, instruments, tones, and volume, which not only is an accurate portrayal of the true essence of what I feel but also makes sense to another English-speaking person.

You feel something but you just can't get it out of your mouth. You aren't communicating well. You can't seem to get the other person to understand what you mean. It's frustrating. It's a loss of your voice.

But then you hear a song. Yes, yes!! That is it! That is exactly how I feel. Thank you, Mr. or Ms. Songwriter! It is cathartic. It is a release. It becomes your voice.

The voice of music can be summed up in one word. Connection. It is the connection we make with each other. It is between the songwriter and the listener. The communication is via the poetry of music and lyrics. This voice of music is the connection with a kindred soul. It is a communication sent out to the world. It asks the hidden question "Is anyone else out there?"

I answer, "Yes, I am here and I know what you feel, I have been there and you summed it up perfectly. I don't know how you did it, but you gave my thoughts, my feelings, my pain, my anger, my hurt, my excitement and my love a voice."

I am not alone. I share a connection to someone else. There is someone else who feels and thinks just like me. I am not alone. Isn't that a most important thing to know?

The Chesney Factor

Sometime in 2003, a friend introduced me to the country music mystery that is known as the Kenny Chesney phenomenon. I didn't really get the allure. I mean, really..."She thinks my tractor's sexy"? What the hell is that all about? The only other song I knew was something like, "You had me from Hello." So you borrow a line from Jerry McGuire and call it a song. Blech.

Frankly, I couldn't understand how Chesney could sell out multiple shows in town after town and in less than twenty minutes. My friend couldn't explain it, either. He just told me that I would thank him later and he knew I would love it. He would not settle for less than me loving it, so I was force-fed Chesney tunes until I got it. I couldn't fake it—I really had to prove that I loved the music and had fully subscribed to the so-called phenomenon.

So, I hauled my little butt to the Target music aisle and picked up three CDs. Yes, I like the music; yes, I like the songs. But the strangest and most important thing was the effect that it had on me. His music was the catalyst for me to tell my story.

I connected with the song "Old Blue Chair," and within minutes one day after hearing it, I was literally and figuratively inspired and I HAD to write. I knew exactly what I needed to say. I felt I had to do it, I sat down and eight hours later I had finished a short story entitled, "The Search for the Old Blue Chair." It just came out of me. It flowed from somewhere deep down.

That essay became my vehicle for telling my story in my motivational speaking engagements. I don't speak for a fee and I am not a motivational speaker by trade, it is something that just sort of happened. Over the past ten years, I have been asked to speak at different events. I don't really know why people ask me, they just do. They ask me to speak on motivation or what I have done to be successful in business. Maybe they love my self-deprecating humor and the fact that I don't charge a fee. Maybe they know I love to talk about myself!

This is not a book about Kenny Chesney. It's about his music, his songwriting and most specifically, it is about how it inspired me. See, first it started with "The Search for the Old Blue Chair," next it became another essay inspired by another Chesney song and then the next thing I knew, I was thinking about writing a book entitled "Good Music is Better than Sex." Next thing I knew, I found myself sitting in the Virgin Islands absorbing the Chesney vibe, on the sole mission to finish my book.

It was as if I didn't have a choice in the matter. Some mysterious force was in charge and I was just along for the ride. There was all this stuff inside of me that needed to come out and Chesney's music released it.

I found my voice through his music.

Oh! And for the record, I do think his tractor is sexy but (and don't tell him this) my ears still bleed when I hear that "Hello" song. It makes me want to throw up.

For those who aren't familiar with Chesney, St. John and the surrounding islands have become his inspiration. His music and songwriting reflect his passion for the islands. So as I said, it was if I had to come to this specific place to complete my book. There were no ifs, ands or buts, it just was. It was the weirdest thing.

And no, I haven't met Kenny and frankly, I don't really need to meet him. I'm a writer, not a stalker, damn it! He gets enough harassment from the damn paparazzi and over-zealous fans. As for me, I just sent a little thank-you note and left it for him with the girls at Woody's.

Woody's—for some strange, inexplicable reason, Table #5 is now my writing table. My original plan was that I would write from my beautiful, secluded, private villa overlooking Cinnamon Bay and Jost Van Dyke. Nope...didn't work out that way.

The energy pulled me to Woody's Seafood Saloon in Cruz Bay, St. John. So my all-time favorite waitresses in the entire world, Jessica Jones, Kandace Jones, Carolyn Mulloy, Jordan Holt, Michelle Lane, Ann Beugette and Jaimis Huff took care of me by checking on me to see if I needed more water, diet coke, or sugar-free red bull for hours on end several days in a row, while I tapped away on my laptop. Since I mentioned all the girls, I have to mention Chad and Todd, the owners, and Creston and Ben from the kitchen. Did I miss anyone?

Therein lies the crazy irony of this whole story—me, the alcoholic sitting in a bar, writing a book about my life, love and trouble with the Drink. Me, sitting and writing about trouble with love and relationships while drunken guys of all ages hit on me! Me, sitting in a bar, pounding away on a laptop, while all these tourists and locals look at me like I'm a lunatic. Me, smiling widely, and probably idiotically, because I haven't been in the Flow of the Zone for a long freaking time and I haven't been able to write for hours on end, ever.

I am so unbelievably psyched about the state of my life and how far I have come these past two years. 2003 seems like a lifetime ago.

The craziest thing about this whole adventure is that it started with one itty bitty little essay and now I've completed something that I am very proud of and that means so much more to me. Writing this is something that I dreamed of doing for years and years, and now—it's done.

This crazy little island known as St. John has had some amazing effect on me! It completed my transformation. I can say with confidence that I am finally the woman that I have always wanted to be.

I absolutely love this rock! Kenny wrote a song about this place called "Magic." Most people aren't familiar with the song because it is so different from his typical thing. It is my favorite song. There is something magical about this place. I'm glad I got to experience it.

I hope that you enjoy the book. This is my soul on paper. Take care with it and enjoy the ride! Hold on tight!

CHAPTER 1
GOOD MUSIC—JOAN JETT & THE BLACKHEARTS

Good music is better than sex. *Seriously.*

I have had good sex. I've had great sex. Of course, I've also had bad sex. God, hasn't everyone? There has even been some amazing, "Oh. My. God. That was the best sex I have ever had in my life, I actually think I may pass out" sex.

However, I stand behind my statement. No matter how great the sex, the orgasmic feeling is fleeting. Don't get me wrong, it is a great feeling. It is that fabulous culminating ecstasy that rolls in swells and breaks like a tsunami and quite possibly for a woman, can happen five, six, maybe even more that eight, times in a row. Quite pleasant indeed. Herein lies the problem— you remember it the next morning and have a shy little coy smile as you reminisce. You may even have that "afterglow" with the ear-to-ear smile that says, "Oh yes, I did have sex. Oh yes, and it was good."

Give it a couple of hours into the day and it will fade away. Poof! Gone. Vanished, and you have forgotten already how that multiple orgasm felt.

But music lingers. It lingers on the mind, on the lips, in the heart, even in the soul. It can linger for hours. Good music doesn't come with the letdown. It doesn't come with post-coital mixed emotional state.

How many women recognize this post-sex internal headache? "Whew, that was amazing! Now I have to go to the bathroom and pee so I don't get a urinary tract infection and climb back into bed for the obligatory cuddle that my mate will give me, only for him to then fall asleep and heave me over to my side of the bed and shove his cold ass in my back while I lay there staring at the ceiling wondering why he couldn't have even muttered 'I love you' during the five-minute spooning session!"

Good music can put me into a pure state of transcendental bliss for hours on end. Days, even. It is *soooooo* much better than sex.

Music is the fabric of my life, it is the soundtrack to the memories of my past, it is the background noise in all I do and it is the poetry of my heart. It can bring me to tears, it can make me feel powerful, it can tap into my anger and it can soothe my soul.

I am a very emotional person and music is my release. It digs deeper into my heart, into my soul, and into my essence as a living, breathing, feeling human being more than anything else in this world.

It is the lyrics, the voice, the guitars, the ethereal feeling that a song can transcend through me and just make me feel. I connect to songs in a way that I am unable to define. It just is, and it makes me free.

In the book, *The Tao of Pooh*, the author, Benjamin Hoff, agrees with me that the principles of music and living are not that different from each other.

"Wouldn't you say, Pooh?"

"Say what?" asked Pooh, opening his eyes.

"Music and Living."

"The same thing," said Pooh.

So there it is. If Pooh says it is so, then it must be so.

Now back to this argument that I am trying to make. Music better than sex? What? I have people look over my shoulder and read the title and say, loudly and very emphatically, "Maybe for you, sister, but not me!"

This profound insight hit me as I was driving solo on Highway 64 east headed towards Nags Head this past spring. Picture this—I am driving along, sun shining, a fabulous 64 degrees, sunroof cracked up, back window halfway down, butt warmer on, digging the world and singing to my little heart's content with Chesney as my back –up singer on CD. We're singing "I Remember" together and as the song ends I say out loud, "That is some good shit. That is better than sex."

I typically hold extremely analytical discussions in my head on random topics. No, no, these are not audio hallucinations. They are just discussions that I have with myself. Like ya'll don't do it. Please!

So, in my head, I tried to define the attraction and pull this crazy thing has over me. What makes me say good music is better than sex? What is it that is so great?

I didn't really come to a conclusion. But it is a very interesting statement.

I mean, Chesney's voice pretty much always sounds the same on every song. Kind of like a steady, stable foundation. It is consistent, it is strong, and it is comforting. It's sturdy, yet soothing. There is a connection to his music. It's like old faded memories calling my name. He takes me somewhere. I don't know where it is, but wherever it is, I like it and I want to stay.

It's this effervescent feeling that comes over me. The hair rising on my arms when a certain note is hit that just makes my heart ache. I can feel the pain, the longing; it delves into my heart with such accuracy I literally am taken to a different place. My mind leaves this earth, my eyes close and I am transported to a place inside of colors, feelings, emotions and memories of the past, present and future. Music is so emotion-filled for me; there is no other release that can ever take its place. Heartache, longing, anger, bitterness, tears, sobbing, loving and losing—I succumb to the music and I am no longer me. It is an empathetic journey that cannot be explained well enough in mere mortal words to do it justice.

Yes, I know, thinking and comparing the essence of good music versus the essence of good sex is a compelling and difficult argument to make. The depth of an artistic act such as singing, or the poetry of lyrics that make an internal connection to someone miles away, unknown to the artist, is in itself a powerful statement.

The connection and strength of the intimacy and pleasure with a person so close that you can breathe the same breath can just as well bring me to tears and bring a loving feeling so deep in my heart that I think I will explode.

Good music is an emotional escapade that allows my soul to soar among the eagles and dance in the clouds. I believe that art's passion can be found in many different things: graffiti to impressionism to photography, from Thoreau to Cobain to even the country music superstar, Chesney. It is at the sole discretion of the giver and the receiver.

It is a moment of pure freedom—that peace and sense of calm that can only come from within the soul. Freedom, or perhaps better named 'pure bliss,' it is a moment in time that eclipses all boundaries.

It is a moment in time that doesn't depend on another person being totally in sync with me, that very nanosecond in the infinite spectrum of time, in one mutually agreeable location, such as a bed or a table or the floor.

Art and music provide a chance for bliss, which doesn't require a prerequisite of a romantic, intimate and statistical anomaly.

This statistical anomaly is something I'll discuss later on, but Readers, think about this as you go on. Think back; think as hard as you can. Try to name all the times that you have had sex: made love, fucked, done the deed, knocked boots, bumped uglies, whatever you want to call it.

Think hard now—really dig deep. How many times can you say that the sole event of that sexual escapade made you feel totally, absolutely, unbelievably full of pure bliss for longer than, say, an hour a day? Pure bliss, now. Think hard. Pure unequivocal freedom of your soul. Bliss. Sweet amazing bliss.

Well, give it some thought. Put on your favorite song, let your soul be free with it and just be for a little while. Just be with the music. Embrace the music.

Let me know how it works out for you and get back to me. I do guarantee results. Oh, and when the feeling starts to fade, play the song again and again, sing loudly with it, play the air guitar. Go on—really be one with the song! It's good, isn't it?

By the way, I have the utmost respect for anyone who puts his or her heart out there. So critics beware—I don't give a damn what you think. Artists of all kinds should be rejoiced and praised for having the guts, the passion and the balls to put their hearts on the line for the world to see.

Even the guy who took a chance and released an album full of songs that he wrote, songs that were inspired by the life he loves, songs that weren't his typical "shtick," even he should be praised for laying it all out there. A lot of critics bashed the Chesney CD *Be as You Are: Songs from the Old Blue Chair*. Even die-hard fans of Chesney's bashed it.

To Kenny I say this, "Well done, well done indeed." Personally, after I heard the CD I rushed to my dear friend, my Chesney compatriot who had advised me to not waste my money, and I said, quite loudly, "Are you on crack? This is the best stuff he has ever done. This is some good shit."

So there it is. My hypothesis is that good music is indeed better than sex. Bring on the objections. I can already hear the critics trashing my so-called views on the depth of country music. Frankly, the objections don't matter, the criticisms don't matter. It is what it is, and to me it is Fabulous!

Oh, I forgot one other thing I would tell Kenny about the critics of the world: "Fuck 'em."

So, as I said many, many paragraphs ago there is this part in that song that just puts me in a good place. There are other songs too, other artists as well. If you ever ride with me on a Specific Adventure, I will point it out to you. It's usually just a clip of a second, a lick of a guitar, or a note that the singer hits and draws out. But don't worry; I'll let you know when it's coming up. Then I'll close my eyes and say with a blissful smile on my face, "That is some good shit. That is better than sex."

***

Yes, I seek solace and shelter in music. Those who can't write music or sing well are left to just enjoy. I enjoy it to the fullest. I like to consider myself a connoisseur of all things music.

My musical education began at a very early age. My brother is a drummer and has played in a band since he was probably 16. Today he is 46, 10 years older than me, and still plays daily. As a drummer for a death metal band (yes, death metal, not just regular heavy metal but a fierce, more aggressive genre known as "death" metal) he first led me gently into musical kindergarten with an introduction to The Beatles.

I can remember as a little girl, probably four at the time, being quizzed on who was who in The Beatles. Frankly, I had a hard time distinguishing between Ringo and George. Give me a break, it was the 70s and they all had long hippie hair. They looked alike.

Later on, when I was in maybe second or third grade, when asked what I went as for Halloween, I had to explain the fact that Alice Cooper is not a female to my teacher. I was supposed to go as a witch…but my brother's love of metal came out. I even had the make-up done perfectly and yes, quite accurately. Whatever, candy is candy.

As a teen, when my brother caught me roller-skating to disco, more specifically, The Bee Gees, I was severely reprimanded for listening to "god-awful crap." At the time, I just liked to do the backward skate to Andy Gibb. What the hell did I know?

"Eclectic" does not even begin to define my taste. My love for all things music covers all spectrums. You name the genre and I can name my favorites. You name the artist and I, most likely, will have a strong opinion on his or her career choice. My musical menagerie ranges from Andrea Bochelli to Motley Crüe; Ludacris to John Tesh; and yes, of course, Kenny Chesney.

My brother and I have had some very in-depth debates regarding our musical differences. But, I agree to disagree with him. Him? Not so much. In fact, when he finds out about this book I will endure the wrath of rock and roll. Chuck, stage name in the 70s Chief Wild Rock, will most certainly attack my views on Chesney and country music as a whole. But I will not mind his spew of criticisms. From my big brother, I was given the best gift in the world. The gift of music. That makes it all worthwhile.

Besides, what other chick do you know that has Barry Manilow, Nine Inch Nails, Chris Cagle, The Cure and Bing Crosby all nicely organized in one little iPod? Viva la iPod!

Speaking of this most magnificent piece of technology, I absolutely love my iPod. Good lord, how have I walked the earth before? This tiny little piece of metal, held in my hand, so small, yet so magnanimous. I feel a love for my iPod that I have never known before. It is, oh how do I describe it? It is almost unearthly. It makes me want to quote Shakespeare.

This tiny little black and silver creature that I cradle in my hand and lovingly caress holds my vast musical library. Should something happen to my little friend, I fear I could no longer live. Or at least live happily.

I have come to grow so dependent on my wee little auditory addiction. So in love with this little manna from heaven, I even pay for my downloads! Just yesterday I spent over $70 solely on Chris Cagle. Oh, iPod and Chris Cagle, how I do love you so…let me count the ways...

21 ways to shake my ass to Hip Hop old school favorites such as Rob Base, DJ EZ Rock, 2 Live Crew & Quad City DJ's.

33 reasons to dream of Chris Cagle. As if a reason was really ever needed! I'd be lying if I said he was not the sexiest man who has ever walked the face of this earth. He sings, he writes songs, he takes pictures and he embraces his inner redneck, just like me! Most importantly, he knows how to spell the word "ya'll" correctly. Please refer to the song "Hey Ya'll." Only true rednecks know how to spell that elusive word and that is quite simply how he won my love. Did I mention that the misspelling of the word ya'll is my number one pet peeve in life? For the record, it is not y'all—it is ya'll. If you're not country, don't even bother trying it. At least Chris gets me!

57 ways to hear Gary Allan, who is the most overlooked country singer and hopefully is soon to claim his due. Gary, you had me at "Drinkin' Dark Whiskey" and a couple of years ago you moved from complete unknown straight to the number three spot on the "Judy Core Top 3 Singers of All Times" list. For the record, tequila does not make my clothes fall off but your unbelievably kick-ass guitar playing on "Putting My Misery on Display" does make my clothes fall off. You have had me for some time now.

101 ways to rock out to the Hard and Loud Playlist. Oh, Scott Weiland, I am so glad you are back in action! Velvet Revolver brings tears to my eyes— tears of joy! Combining the boys of G-n-R with your ragged, angst-filled, subtle yet amazingly powerful voice… it is a most magnificent idea! It is the most magnificent thing to happen to music in a long while. The state of the rock music scene breaks my heart, but you Scott Weiland, you bring me hope. I am so glad you are still alive. I don't quite understand *how* you are still alive, but damn it—I'm glad.

Let me count the ways that I love you, oh little iPod of mine. The ways that I love you total 1394, yes 1394 songs that I can carry in my back pocket. Never fear, dear iPod, you little vixen you, I will continue to download until I have maxed out your capacity!

You, dear iPod, you are my soul mate.

CHAPTER 2
BLACK—PEARL JAM

Okay. C'mon, let's go on this beautiful journey called life! Bring your Kleenex, because there are some sad, weepy moments. You need some psychosocial background information about me to catch you up to speed. It will give you context and help you understand me a little better.

Born on November 28, 1969 to Barb and Del Core in Tampa, Florida, was a precious little bundle of joy to be named Judith Marie Core. Marie is my grandmother's name and it is a Core thing: at least one girl born to a Core must have the middle name "Marie." I have a sister 12 years older and a brother 10 years older and no, I wasn't a freaking mistake and how unbelievably rude of people to even say that to me. (It was my brother, not me— I was "planned"). Grew up in middle class suburbia, not rich, not poor, but yes, my clothes did come from the Sears catalog and yes, it sucked.

The prized possessions of my youth included but are not limited to the following: my Barbie dream house, Barbie corvette, pink huffy bike, and Curious George. I had glasses in 5th grade, which then moved me several rungs down the social ladder. I had buckteeth and sucked my thumb till I was 10 or maybe even 13. Apparently my capitalist nature won out and I was bribed to cease the sucking with a pair of skates. I still have not received my red devil wheels. Hello?? Shall I expect them anytime soon??

I grew up in the church. My social life was filled with church stuff. Sunday school, regular service, youth group, church choir, Wednesday night Bible studies, lock ins in Gage Hall, Youth Week, church camp. Yes, there was something going on all the time. All my friends were friends from the youth group.

I never saw my parents fight; I think my dad may have been a mute, and my mother could have stopped Hitler with "the look." You know, that fabulous, "You have disappointed me and have not done as I believe you should have and therefore you are going to hell. You are not even worthy of my wrath: in fact, I will act as if you don't exist" look. I would have rather had the switch a million times than get "the look."

As a teenager, I vividly remember feelings of confusion. Not confusion over hormones, boys or uncontrollable "teenage feelings," but confusion within my own head. I remember not really knowing who I was, what to say or when to say it. I can still recall the uncertainty I faced each day, not even being sure of myself as a self, not even knowing if what I thought was real. It was as if I were not really in my body, but watching everything around me, not really sure if I were feeling and thinking. All of this confusion left me highly anxious. I threw up all the time. I had panic attacks daily and I hated school immensely.

I had confusion over how I was supposed to act around boys. In seventh grade I ran a race against a boy named Wade. All my little girlfriends told me that I better not win because the boy wouldn't like me. I won anyway.

What was wrong with me the way that I was? Why couldn't I be demure, quiet, and be the "perfect girl" like the other little girls? I was always told I was too loud, too outspoken, too much. "Judy, lower your voice, people can hear you." "Be nice, be quiet, be sweet." "Guys don't like girls who cuss." "You should be flirty—guys don't like it when you tell them they are wrong about something." "Maybe you should try to tone it down a bit."

I wasn't right the way that I was. I needed to be different than who I was, I needed to be what everyone else told me was right. I needed to be liked. I needed to be accepted. I needed to fit in.

Be something else, be something better. Be something different. Guys won't like you as you are. Be something else.

I tried to tone it down. I tried to be the girl that guys liked in high school. I tried. Justin told me to wear skirts and be more girly, to be like the other girls. I wore skirts. I tried to be more girly. I wore makeup. I tried to not be as loud. I tried.

Something happened during my last few weeks of high school. I "blossomed." I had lost my baby fat and my chest expanded. I became a 36C. All of a sudden I was the girl that guys liked.

It did not take a degree in neuropsychology for me to correlate the increase in male attention was in direct proportion to the increase in my bra size. All of a sudden guys who didn't acknowledge my presence while walking the same hallways for the past three years started talking to me. It took me a while, but soon I wasn't flattered. I was just pissed off. I was the same person I had always been. And they, they were very apparent.

Because of the disappointing status of our social lives in 9th grade, Michelle Miller and I had created imaginary boyfriends for ourselves. Mine was named Cappy. He was a surfer with blonde hair and blue eyes. He was gorgeous and he adored me. I don't remember Michelle's imaginary guy, but he was Cappy's best friend, he drove a Jeep Wrangler and we all hung out together. These daydream plots were very elaborate and this dream lasted well into high school.

On June 7, 1987, I met Cappy, only his name turned out to be Donald James Butler and he lived in Lakeland, Florida. He was 19 and went by "Donnie." He liked to talk to me and he thought I was funny and smart. It wasn't about my chest and it wasn't about sex.

I met him in Daytona at Beach Week. We dated and after a couple of months I wanted Donnie to be my first. I wanted to have sex with him. This was not a decision that I had just made at the spur of the moment, it was something that I had thought long and hard about and I felt that it was the right decision for me. He asked me if I was sure and I was absolutely without a doubt sure of this decision.

I remember the way he smelled, his tan skin, his blonde hair and his beautiful blue eyes. I remember his laugh, his throaty voice and his arm around my neck. I remember making out in the backseat of his baby blue 1965 Mustang with the front license plate that had a swirl of colors and an outline of a surfer in the middle. I remember us lying by the pool in Daytona gazing at each other from across the deck. I remember him pulling his sunglasses down in his Risky Business imitation. I remember how he wrote "Donnie loves Judy" with a heart around it in the sand. Then the waves washed half of it away.

I remember every single detail of every minute with him in 1987.

It was not the right decision for my parents. Due to teenage stupidity, sneaking out, lying about my whereabouts and my car breaking down on an interstate, the truth surfaced and all hell broke loose in my house. They made me break up with him on the phone. I couldn't leave the house except to go to work and they tracked the mileage on my car. I was not to ever see him again.

I didn't. Two years later, by complete random circumstances, I found out he had gotten heavily into drugs and committed suicide. I don't know what happened in his life or how it had gotten that bad. I couldn't bring myself to call his parents. All I could do was cry. I cried for him, I cried for me and I cried for the loss of my dream.

I had self-esteem issues. I had trust and abandonment issues. I had closure issues. Last but not least, the veil in which my depression, sadness, loss and insecurity was shrouded in—anger issues.

Anger ate me alive. I was a very, very, very angry young woman. Angry at my parents, angry at life, angry at Donnie, angry at God, angry at anyone or anything that got in my way.

Very quickly, I transitioned from the invisible girl with glasses and braces in high school to the Larger than Life Blonde Creature. You've probably seen her. You can't miss her...pissed off, big hair, loud mouth, short skirts and big boobs, life of the party. She might be telling someone to fuck off, she might be dancing sandwiched between two guys, she might be making out with some stray at the bar...trust me, you've seen her.

Dancing on a bar, dancing on a table in a bar, getting in a fight with someone in a bar, being tossed out of a bar, throwing up in a garbage can in a bar, waking up hung over next to some guy she met in a bar, driving home from a bar with one eye closed to stay between the lines....

The blur of 1988—1994 can be pieced together as follows:

I went to University of South Florida full time and moved out on my own because I hated being at home. I lived in an apartment in the 'hood of Tampa. I moved about a million times and my front door was constantly revolving with roommates. I lost count many years ago.

I worked full time to pay for my independence. Fuck them; I didn't need those people trying to tell me what to do and how to be. I was anxious all the time. Not really feeling comfortable in my own body. Being who I thought I was supposed to be. Fun, life of the party, the good-time girl, put the mask on. Don't let anyone see the truth. Panic attacks while driving on the highway.

Drinking, drinking, drinking...drinking till I couldn't feel. Burying feelings, deep, deeper, getting drunk again and starting all over again.

I had quite a volatile love-hate relationship with this Obnoxious Drunk Blonde Creature. Life as the Creature is wonderful—all of the pain miraculously goes away!!! It's wonderful; she's the life of the party, guys think she is awesome because she can drink them under the table, and she is sexy because she dances on top of the bar, and she is a bad ass!!! Plus, she is amazing in bed!!! She knows no inhibitions! She is invincible!! Fun, fun, fun, she is nothing but pure, off-the-hook fun!!! She'll buy everyone drinks! She does shots with strangers, she lets hot guys do body shots off her stomach! Everybody loves her!!!

Ah yes—then the lights come on…and she doesn't want it to end. So she drinks more, and more, and more.

Then somewhere in between the darkness and the light the Creature fades to black and I reappear. I feel like shit. What happened? I try to piece blocks of time together. I remember dancing. I think I did a shot or two. I was drinking with some guys. I remember something about a guy in a black shirt. I went to the bathroom…did I throw up in a garbage can? I don't remember. Why am I naked? Oh shit, who the hell is he? How did I get home? I don't remember! Oh shit.

My confusion turns to anger and I begin to lash out at the Blonde Creature…"You are a fucking slut," "Who the hell is this guy?" "What did you do?" "You are such a fucking whore." Anger turns to pain and pain turns to tears.

I'd beat myself up mentally with guilt, embarrassment and self-hatred for the Blonde Creature. What the hell is wrong with me? Why can't I control her? Why do I keep letting this happen? What the fuck is wrong with me?

Run. Run. Just get your ass up out of this bed and get the hell out of this house. I would yell at myself and begin the internal attack on myself. Once I found my car, I would drive. Drive as fast as I could to get away. Sobbing hysterically through rivers of tears, my face swollen and red, I would weave in and out of traffic trying to get home as fast as I could. What will I say to my friends? Oh God, did I get in a fight with someone? I don't know.

Pretend like it didn't happen. Just pretend like nothing happened. Pretend like nothing is wrong. Do not say a word to anyone. I won't let this happen again. I won't do this again. I won't drink anymore. I won't drink. I won't drink. I will have more control next time. Next time. Next time.

There was always a next time.

Here are some mathematical calculations—I was 17 when I started college. I was in school for 7 years (give me a break, I changed majors). Going out a minimum of 5 nights a week for 7 years—that's about 1800 days of this cycle. Oh, but it didn't end at graduation. Of course not. I got a real job, and instead of going out 5 nights a week, it was downsized to 2 nights for another 2 years.

Kasey's Kove; Brahaus, which became CC's; Patrick's; Harpo's in Ybor; Irish Pub; Green Iguana, both locations; Killian's on Waters Avenue then Killian's in Ybor; Sydney's, which became Stingray's on Fowler; CDB's Restaurant on Friday nights; Yucatan Liquor Stand in Westshore; Baja Beach Club; Masquerade; Despoparados; American Cowboy; Jelly Rolls; Blues Ship; Carmine's, bar, after bar, after bar, day after day, year after year.

Love the Creature. Hate the Creature. Love the Creature. Hate the Creature. Hate the Creature, hate, hate, hate the Creature.

CHAPTER 3
OLD BLUE CHAIR—KENNY CHESNEY

Old Blue Chair ("Be as You Are" Version)"—Kenny Chesney

There's a blue rocking chair
Sittin in the sand
Weathered by the storms and well oiled hands
It sways back and forth with the help of the winds,
Seems to always be there, like an old trusted friend
I've read a lot of books,
Wrote a few songs
Looked at my life where it's goin, where it's gone
I've seen the world through a bus windshield, but nothing compares
To the way that I see it,
to the way that I see it,
to the way that I see it when I sit in that old blue chair
From that chair I've caught a few fish and some rays
And I've watched boats sail in and out of cinnamon bay
I let go of a lover that took a piece of my heart
I prayed many times for forgiveness and a brand new start
I've read a lot of books,
Wrote a few songs
Looked at my life where it's goin, where it's gone
I've seen the world through a bus windshield, but nothing compares
To the way that I see it, to the way that I see it,
to the way that I see it when I sit in
that old blue chair
That chair was my bed one New Year's Night
When I passed out from too much Cruzan and Diet
And woke up to a hundred mosquito bites,
I swear got 'em all sittin right there
In that old blue chair
There's a blue rockin chair
Sittin' in the sand
Weathered by the storms and well oiled hands

I remember when I first heard the song "Old Blue Chair." March 2004. He was so damn lucky. He had found it—he had found the secret. He found that small minuscule fragment that is needed to make sense of this vast sea of life.

Damn that Kenny Chesney—how did he do it?

He found what I have been looking for all my life and he found it in something as simple as an old blue chair. A place of peace, serenity, a place that provided the quiet in a desperate storm, the sanctuary, the refuge that I spent all of my life searching for, and he found it in an old blue rocking chair.

Okay, let's speak frankly here. No, I have not literally been scouring the earth for a blue rocking chair. It's a metaphor. Okay, clarification—for Kenny it really is an old blue rocking chair sitting in the sand on Peter Bay in St. John. For me, it's a metaphor. All of my life I have been seeking a place of comfort. A place to just be, just be me, a place that provides the safety and comfort of an old trusted friend, a place that makes me warm inside, makes me feel sane in an insane world. A place where all the chaos is left behind and all that takes over is the quiet of the mind and the soft gentle caressing chorus of the waves.

Remember when we were little…remember our "binkies," "blankies," "woogies?" Remember those? Remember those torn little bits of blankets we dragged around? They were worn and ragged, but they carried the salt of our tears, the slime from our runny noses and the slobber from when we slept with our mouths wide open.

They were magical—they brought us comfort, safety and security in a dangerous world filled with big people and scary unknowns. This magical piece of fabric protected us from the monsters under our bed, provided high-level mass security against the ever-evil bogeyman that was lurking in our closet.

Remember as we got older? We made forts—and of course no man or beast alive could penetrate the protective cover of kitchen chairs in a circle covered by a queen-size bed comforter. We were safe—we could crawl into our secret fort and no one could see us, no one could find us and no one would dare enter our sacred space. We could play with our imaginary friends, hold deep conversations with our stuffed animals, and no one could pass judgment, because we were protected by the impenetrable force of the "fort."

As a pre-teen I had the Kit-Kat Klub. This secret society that consisted of me and Stephanie Kojima held our covert, clandestine meetings in our maximum-security clubhouse in my backyard. If you were not a member you were not allowed to cross the threshold. It was dark little building, probably from Sears, and it may have been yellow on the outside and may have had flowers on it, and quite possibly had an easy-bake oven in the kitchen, but it was hallowed ground. And no one, no one, I said, was allowed inside. Secret things could be said, secret fears could be revealed, whispers about boys, hushed tones about boobs, periods and deodorant….Those walls provided safety from the scary world of "becoming a woman." The Kit Kat Klub ruled!

I don't know where my playhouse is anymore. I think it may have been home to the mower and the weed whacker after the Kit Kat Klub disbanded. Most recently it was replaced by an aluminum-sided utility building that is my dad's woodworking shop.

I don't play in a fort anymore. I don't have my binkie. I so desperately need one.

***

I went home for Christmas 2003 as a newly-separated, going-on-twice-divorced 34 year old, recently booked for a DWI, fired from a job where I was top producer, and overall pretty much a freaking loser whose personal life looked like the carnage from a train wreck.

Hello, my name is Judy and I am a big fat loser who has absolutely nothing except two ex-husbands, an alcohol detector ignition device in my car, a student loan that had amassed to an un-godly amount of money due to an unfinished doctoral program, two cats that drive me nuts and a puppy named Maisy who fills the void unfilled by my lack of a baby. Yes, that is me. Happy fucking birthday to me! All my childhood dreams came true!

I like to think that I am an over-achiever and that is why I had my mid-life crisis at 34 versus 50.

***

Let's go back to 1995. One day, I wake up and I am 26.

Nine years of being "not girlfriend material," two years with a verbally abusive coke addict, seven years of hook ups, one night stands, three months with this guy, two months with that guy…. Partying with the PiKapps and the SAE's, partying with the Busch Garden/Adventure Island crowd, sex here, sex there…

Nine years of hating the Blonde Creature. Nine years of trying to kill the Creature. After nine years I had given up fighting with her. The Creature won. She had taken over. She was me and I was her.

I met my first husband through a group of mutual friends in 1995. He once told me that the first time he saw me was at a party my roommates and I had thrown. Apparently, his best friend told him that I was out of his league and to not even think about it.

So he moved into the Circle of Friends. Quiet and funny, he was a really good guy. Reliable, loyal, and a good listener, he was all the things that allow heterosexual guys to enter into the Circle of Friends. We started dating and three months later we were engaged.

I remember trying to break up at one point prior to the engagement. I started to…but his voice and the voices of all my friends, my family and his family drowned out my voice. "He is a great guy," "He loves you," "You always go for assholes," "You are self-destructive," "Why can't you just be with a nice guy?" "You're an idiot if you fuck this up," "If something happens between the two of you, we'll keep him and get rid of you"…

From the time that we got engaged to the time we separated I had gone from 115 pounds to 165 pounds. The Drunk Blonde Creature had morphed into the "Married Woman." I stopped dressing like a hooch. I stopped dancing on bars, I didn't go out with the girls anymore, I didn't talk with the guys anymore, I tried to stop cussing, I stopped fighting, I became more compliant—I held all the anger inside.

Smile, smile, nod, nod. "Yes, yes, everything is great," "Yes, I'm so very lucky," "Yes, I am so very happy." Smile some more. Laugh. Smile and nod some more.

You would have thought the drinking would stop, huh? No, no—in fact, it got worse. Everything was a drinking occasion for the two of us. We may not have been going to bars, but that didn't stop the drinking. On Wednesday's "The Drew Cary Show" came on— a fabulous reason to drink!

One night, I was so drunk I passed out on the floor of the cats' bathroom and couldn't find my way out of the room. Oh yes, sad and very pathetic, but painfully true. And yes, the cats had their own bathroom.

I was married, I had a great guy who loved me, why was I still so unhappy? That emptiness inside me would reverberate louder and louder. There is no other way to describe it other than to think of a large empty void within.

What the hell was wrong with me? Why couldn't I be happy? So did I discuss this with him, go to marriage counseling, even just go to individual therapy? Of course not. I held it all inside for two years until I thought I was going to explode, and then I dumped it on him and did the only thing I was good at—I ran and hid.

I didn't have a fort to run and hide in, and the Kit Kat Klub was gone, so I did what most adults do—they run to someone else. And I did.

Ahh, sweet bliss once again! The happiness, the excitement of falling in love again, the newness, the high of being in love, finding my soul mate, having someone to confide in, gazing into each others eyes…. Ahh, the feelings mean I am alive, the high is so wonderful I don't want to ever come down.

Ah…but guess what? I eventually came down. Those problems in marriage #1 that I thought were tied to husband #1 become the same problems in marriage #2. But why, how could this be??? He is my soul mate, he completes me, he is My Everything, and he is perfect for me.

Yet I was still me. And the Blonde Creature was still alive.

I wasn't drinking every night anymore. I had lost all my weight. I was in love, I was happy, I was full. So I thought. Slowly, the need to drink crept back up on me. Slowly but surely, the Blonde Creature would start making special appearances again.

I found myself picking up a bottle of wine to drink while watching TV for the weekends that he was gone with his kids. There I was swinging by the grocery store because I had a bad day so I needed a six-pack to chill out.

Always making excuses. Always finding excuses. Always having a reason to drink. Always needing an excuse to drink.

I said to myself "Oh, I'll only drink one or two." Then I was out and I needed to run to the store for more.

A six-pack became a twelve-pack. The little four-pack of individual bottles of wine became the largest bottle of wine. One glass of wine would become two. Two became a bottle. A bottle would be enough to pass out.

There were lots of bad days at work, lots of good reasons to go out afterward for drinks. I'd have six vodka & cranberry drinks in a two-hour time frame after work with friends. Oh, but I didn't want it to end. The Blonde Creature refused to let fun end. The night could never just end quietly.

"C'mon on, let's go party somewhere!!! Let's keep going!!! I'll buy! I'll drive, c'mon, c'mon!!! I'm stressed, let's get fucked up! I'm happy, let's get fucked up! I'm depressed, let's get fucked up! I'm buying, drinks on me!"

And so the story goes….

Fast forward again. October 2002, Husband #2 and I are fired from our jobs (we worked together) due to a coup led by a man that we both trusted and respected. I was bitter and could not believe something like this could happen. Emotionally, I had major issues with trust, betrayal and the realization that my judge of character was askew. I grieved being fired from a job. I was the top producer. How could this happen? What about all the money I made for the company? What about all the hours I worked? The weekends? I busted my ass for five years straight and this is what I get in return? Confused, I could not make sense of what had happened. Fired. No severance package. No severance package for my husband. Promises made by others. Promises broken.

We started a new company and very tough and difficult times followed. Financially, we were broke. We refinanced our cars, sold our house, cashed out our 401k's. Emotionally, we dealt with the litigation we were pulled into, dealt with numerous depositions, attacks by lawyers, rumors and gossip, dealt with the grief of watching the company we had both worked so hard for go down the drain because some group of idiots thought they knew how to run a business.

This story in itself is a painful, dramatic ride. I don't want to go into every detail because that is not what this book is about. However, I do want to emphasize the damage it did to me, my husband, our boss, his wife and his son. It ultimately led to the death of a multi-million dollar company.

If you have ever been deposed, you know it is not a fun experience. Lawyers attack you, say horrible things about you, and ask you intimate questions about your personal life. They attack your competence, integrity and character. Case in point, the lawyer deposing me accused me of lying, incompetence and unethical behavior. He even asked me questions about my husband and my sex life. And that is why I hate lawyers.

So that is another book for a later date. It is a book of greed, lies and why I hate lawyers, which perhaps I will title "The Lying Mother Fuckers at A Large Unnamed Bank and the Lies They Told and the Unethical Things They Did and Why The Large Unnamed Bank is a Den of Thieves that Sues a 65-Year-Old Man and his Wife, and Their Son, Sent the Family into Bankruptcy and Ruined Three Companies in the Meantime, All After the 65-year-old Man Made Over 450 Million Dollars in Tax Credits for the Big Evil Bank."

Then perhaps I will write a sequel and entitle it, "If You are a Bank and You are Going to Buy an Affordable Housing Real Estate Development Company Because You Need the CRA Credit Because You are a Bank Known for Redlining in Atlanta, Then You Might Want to Know That if You Sue the People That Ran the Company for You and Made You Millions of Dollars, You Might Need to Understand a Little Bit About How Business Works Because You Will Look Like Dumbasses When You Depose People Like Judy Core and She Will Tell You That You Are a Dumbass."

Okay, sorry for the little editorial side bar there. *After almost two and half years of litigation and the deposing of over 30 people, the litigation was settled and, without naming names, the large unnamed Bank had to pay $250,000 to the parties whose lives were dragged through hell because of the two greedy lying mother fuckers whose names I won't name, but if you really want to know who they are, give me a call!* I'm still a wee bit bitter, does it show?

Moving along, there was a teensy weensy little incident involving the law. I got a DWI in January 2003. Apparently, 14 large glasses of Shiraz, cab and merlot on an empty stomach will result in a BAC of .18. Yeah, that is pretty high. The judge asked me how I was still standing, much less driving. I don't know. I was blacked out.

The bad times had only just begun. The axis of my globe was yanked away and my world crashed to the ground. Shattered, irreparable pieces of my life lay submerged, drowned in a pool of alcohol, vomit, and a triple shot of self-loathing.

I did stop drinking—for one month. That was the hardest, longest thirty days of my life. I did the rationalizing, I did the denial: I did have a drinking problem, but it was something I could control. I just wouldn't drink and drive. I could drink in a "safe" environment. Yeah, that's it…a safe environment. It's like that old joke: I got arrested for drinking and driving, so I did what any rational person would do. I gave up driving.

Then the drinking started all over again. Unlike my first husband, my second husband was not a big partier. Plus, with my recent run in with the Raleigh Police Department, I felt his judging eyes weigh down on me. He never said anything, but I could feel what he was thinking. So, I had to make a more concerted effort to keep my alcohol activities more covert.

I couldn't wait till he went out of town so I could just chill out in front of the TV with a big bottle of wine. Just to give you an example of what stupid things you do when you are under the influence, I actually watched the movie "Glitter" one drunken Friday night. The whole movie. Yep, two hours of my life gone. I must confess something else, as if that in itself is not bad enough I actually shed some tears when Mariah Carey's DJ boyfriend got killed. Damn that alcohol. Damn you, you spawn of Satan.

When my husband was around I would look for opportunities for us to go to dinner so I could have a drink. If we did Italian, I could have red wine, if we went Mexican, I could have sangria. I had it all planned out. All planned out. My tidy little drinking agenda.

Times were bad. And then bad went to worse and worse went to hell.

We had the stress of the lawsuit, dealing with lawyers, being deposed, a new company trying to make payroll, we were broke, our savings gone and he was so stressed out I expected him to drop dead of a heart attack at any minute. As for me, I would just drink and curl up into a little mental fetal position.

Our marriage of only a year and a half was teetering on the brink of death and I pushed it over the edge. I did what I do best (second to drinking). I hate confrontation, I abhor conflict, so I held all my emotions inside and swam around in a deep sea of depression and then it blew. The tidal wave of depression had consumed me. I couldn't see above the waves anymore. All I knew was that I was unhappy and wanted to die.

Ironically, the day it blew happened to be November 2, 2003. Ask me what day it all came to a head with Husband #1? Go ahead, ask. November 2, 1998.

I think God has a sense of humor and perhaps a love for the dark comedy of life. It was very clear to me that God, in all his glory and irony, said, "If you can't get it right the first time, let's do it again. You can keep running but you can't keep hiding."

We separated because I knew that I needed to conquer these demons on my own. No one else was going to make them go away. No one was going to fill the void and no one else could make me happy. I had to face the void head on. I had to fix me before I did any more damage to those around me, those I loved and those who loved me.

CHAPTER 4
TURN YOU INSIDE—OUT—R.E.M.

It was time to begin the journey of self-exploration, self-understanding and ultimately self-acceptance. Someone wise once said you only change when the fear of staying the same is greater than the fear of change. The scale had finally tipped. I needed to change.

It's easy now to look back and see everything so clearly. Back then I couldn't see two inches in front of me, I couldn't hear my own voice and I didn't even know what I did know and did not know.

I couldn't even really make sense of what was in my own head, much less try to describe it to a therapist. There were no words, just all these feelings swirling around, consuming me and engulfing me.

Mush person. Those were the words I used to describe myself. I felt like a mush person. I used to be such a strong, confident woman in my professional life, but in my personal life, I was a mush person. Just a big pile of mush, no thoughts, no opinions, no idea of up or down. Just mush.

I was like a pendulum. One day I would swing one way, the next day I would swing to the opposite side. There was never any happy medium. The pendulum was always swinging. It would never stay on one side for too long. Just as I got comfortable with it being on the left side, the pendulum would abruptly swing to the right with no warning.

I couldn't live like this anymore. I needed someone to help me and I had to stick with it. Flipping through the pages, I called a psychologist. She graduated from Duke, so she had to be pretty smart. Plus, she took my insurance.

I started therapy in October 2003. I went two times a week every week. It was a very rough ride. I pretty much just sat on a couch and cried for an hour each session.

I would leave her office feeling worse than when I went in. It seemed that my list of issues was so long, it was amazing that I had not been institutionalized at some point earlier in my life. God, I really was fucked up. I mean, she did graduate from Duke and she thought I was fucked up.

We made a list of my goals. I needed to get my drinking under control, because again, it was a depressant and people who are really depressed don't need more depressants. I needed to get my emotions and moods under control, most likely on medication. Maybe I needed to be in group therapy with a bunch of strangers openly confronting each other with our unconscious behaviors that are self-destructive and attention-seeking. I needed to not be in a relationship because my issues with the man in my life were not really with him, they were some unconscious need that was unfulfilled as a child and he probably had no idea that I had such unhappiness inside and that the divorces probably came as a complete surprise to both ex-husbands. I had a romanticized view of love and marriage and really didn't know what commitment meant. I needed to learn to be able to be by myself because no one else could fulfill my needs. I had poor self-esteem; I viewed myself as incompetent, worthless, stupid, and a bad person. I was constantly seeking out validation in others. Oh, and most importantly, I needed to grow up.

Ouch. Talk about tough love. I mean, when you're at the bottom and you feel like shit, maybe you don't necessarily need to hear all that stuff about yourself. There would be lots of bumps, bruises and punches to the gut during this journey.

There are three key life moments to highlight during part one of the journey. One moment drove me to the Edge, one pushed me over the Edge and the final moment was the rope that pulled me out from the depths of the Edge.

The first key moment is known as the "Pit of Despair." On January 16, 2004, I went out with a bunch of friends and got very drunk: *shocking*! In my typical fashion of continuing the party all night long, I had mapped out on a napkin (which still exists) a travel plan—we were going to fly into Miami, party at the Clevelander on South Beach, drive to Tavernier, party at the Tiki Bar and then head down to Key West for a couple of days. We would also hit the Dry Tortugas for some diving. Oh yes, it was all planned. I was even so drunk when I got home I checked for tickets. I apparently had pledged to foot the bill for this trip for four girls. It was a long, hard night of drinking.

I woke up the next morning. I awoke in the Pit of Despair. Alcohol is a depressant. Remember I mentioned that earlier? According to Dr. Alexander it is probably not very good for a person who is already incredibly depressed.

How do I describe this to someone who has never been in the Pit? It is uncontrollable sobbing, hard chest-pounding convulsions, not being able to breathe because the sobs are coming over you like a tidal wave that never ends. And it is black, pitch black, the blackest black you can possibly imagine. You can't see in front of you. All you can feel is pain eating you alive and drowning you in blackness. You can't even explain why you are crying, it just hurts so bad. It is unfathomable, unimaginable and indescribable. The pain, the emptiness and the blackness just hurt so incredibly bad you just want it to stop at all costs.

This is where the pain becomes so unbearable that it has eaten out your heart, soul and mind. You cannot think; you can only feel the blackness of the pain. And that is where you would rather take the plunge into death than continue on with the pain. Because it really is that bad. It is black. Nothing but endless black encompassing you. Just black. Hideous blackness.

Let me frankly state something about depression and suicide. I detest, I Hate, when people say something like, "Suicide is so stupid," "It's the highest form of selfishness," or "What do you have to be depressed about?"

Seriously, I truly think that these people mean well, but they missed that day in class where the teacher taught empathy. The problem is that while perhaps their comments might be based in some horribly misconstrued sense of uncompassionate fear of the unknown, they are mainly based in ignorance of mental illness and subsequently, depression.

I couldn't just snap out of it. For me, thinking about ending it all, committing suicide, was the only way to stop the pain. I didn't necessarily want to die. I just wanted the pain to stop. It hurt that unbelievably bad. There was nothing but pain and black. Stop the hurt. Stop the blackness. Because it hurt that bad.

I have never been in that much pain. I couldn't see, I couldn't think. In my blackness, there was a tiny little voice that said "minute by minute, take it minute by minute." I called my therapist and left a sobbing message that I needed help. Fearing that I would pick up a knife and put a final stop to the pain, I forced myself to stay on the couch and not move. Sobbing hysterically, my body so tense it was hard to breathe, clutching the edge of the cushions, I never left the couch. I was scared of myself.

Slowly, nine hours later, the blackness did begin to thin out. I stayed on the couch until Dr. Alexander called me and got me in. I started on Zoloft that day. I don't care about anyone's opinions on mental illness, but it is chemical. It is a brain disorder and it can be treated with medicine. Now, after two years on Zoloft, my moods and emotions are under control. For the first time in my life, I am not at the mercy of my emotions.

According to Dr. Alexander, a lot of people that have addictions have mood disorders. Our addictions are how we manage the ups and downs: that is normal for us. That is how we know we are alive, when we feel.

So, do you think I stopped drinking? Oh, hell no.

The second key moment was June 12, 2004. Somewhere between key moment number one and key moment number two, I stopped seeing Dr. Alexander. I didn't stop taking the Zoloft but I had pretty much convinced myself that as long as I had the Zoloft, who needed therapy? Besides, it made me more depressed to hear all my issues and how unbelievably fucked up I was.

The second key moment is known as the Tim McGraw moment. I went to a concert with some friends, and I was pumped up. I was in my safe environment and was not driving. I was single, looking good if I did say so myself, and ready to party with a capital P.

I got drunk: in fact, I got so drunk the last portion of the concert was a blur. However, I am fairly sure that I told the strangers next to me how much I loved Tim McGraw and how hot he was. I am fairly sure I said this about thirty plus times. I proceeded to get into a fight with my friend Tammy because she would not let the party go on. Even though Lacey was passed out in the back seat, I wanted to go party on at the local country bar, The Longbranch. Tammy nixed that. She knows me well and knew that I had passed a reasonable limit back at the first ten minutes of Tim's set. She is a good friend.

She drove me home and dropped me off in front of my apartment. As I was walking to my door, I looked over to my car and thought to myself, "Well, the alcohol interlock is on the Mitsubishi Spyder, but I could take my brand new Toyota 4 Runner and go get more beer. It doesn't have the interlock!"

No matter how drunk I was, no matter how blacked out I was, I clearly remember thinking, "Fuck. I am a drunk." Fuck, with a capital F. I have a problem. I am an alcoholic and I need help.

I would actually have risked getting arrested again, losing my license and going to jail, all because I wanted more beer. More beer. Beer.

Readers, please let me clarify something. My spyder had the alcohol interlock ignition installed in it. I could not start my vehicle without breathing into it, and it randomly goes off during the hour and then at some point you have to turn it off and turn it back on. If I was caught driving a vehicle without the interlock, I would lose my license and go to jail. If I was caught driving a vehicle without the interlock and had a BAC of more than .04 I would lose my license indefinitely. While the interlock ignition device has been removed now, my driving privileges remain restricted until September 1, 2007.

Needless to say, I cried violently for several days. That is a hard realization to deal with; it is a hard truth to face. Once something like that came out, I couldn't run from it. I couldn't deny it any longer. I was an alcoholic. Not a binge drinker, not an alcohol abuser, but an alcoholic. There just ain't no way to pretty it up. It is what it is and it ain't pretty.

I started my required substance abuse program that week. I haven't had a drink since that night.

My third moment is the rope that pulled me back over the top and away from the edge. It is the Kenny Chesney factor. It may not seem like much, but it is and will always be the most pivotal and important moment in my life.

His concert in Raleigh was July 18, 2004, only a little over a month since I had stopped drinking. It was my first test. I had never attended a "fun, social" event and not drank. Ever. Never in 18 years. Drunk for 18 years. Holy Shit! That is a long time to be drunk. And here I was at a concert with 20,000 plus drunk people. Sober. S-O-B-E-R.

Well, I did it, and it was a monumental occasion for me because it was the first time in my life that I had an awesome, fun time sober. I could be around drinking and I was okay. I didn't need to drink.

I felt liberated, strong, and powerful. I was on my way. I remember how awesome the concert was, I remember being able to sing at the top of my lungs, I remember everything. I was in the moment. I had fun, real honest-to-god fun. Sober. It was possible to have fun without alcohol. Holy shit.

I didn't know who this sober chick named Judy was I had just met her. But damn, she was a fun time with no bad side effects. I liked her. I had to get to know her better. She might even have best friend potential.

I haven't had a drink since June 12, 2004. I have stayed in therapy. I have stayed on Zoloft and I stayed true to my mission of finding my own old blue chair.

It's a journey we must all make on our own. No one can do it for us.

We each find our own way. I had to learn for myself that all the promotions I got, the amount of money I made, the degrees I racked up, the people I filled my life with, the way I look, the color of my hair, the stuff I bought to make me feel better, spending money, or even delving into religious fanaticism does not bring the old blue chair.

The old blue chair is within each of us, but it is a long, hard journey to find it. Just like Kenny says, I too, have looked at my life, where I'm going, where I've gone, and I have prayed for forgiveness and asked for new starts, I've passed out from rum and diet, I've lost lovers that took a piece of my heart.

I've been searching for years. I've searched for answers in the bottom of bottles, searched for answers in the love of others, I've read countless self-help books, I've studied religion and philosophy, searched for answers in academia, looked to others to give me the answers, wandered around on the road of life aimlessly.

I never wanted to look to where the answers really were. They were in the mirror reflecting back at me every day. I didn't want to do the hard work to get there. I was scared. I was afraid.

I've found my old blue chair and you know what? He's got it right. Nothing compares to how I see life when I'm sitting in my old blue chair.

Oh—so you want to know what *my* old blue chair is.

Well here you go. It is driving with the windows down, sun shining in, 76 degrees and I'm singing at the top of my lungs. Sometimes it's two-stepping around my house by myself to a little George Strait. It's riding next to Tammy, both of us singing "Live Like You Were Dying" with Tim McGraw like we're on stage.

Music is my old blue chair.

CHAPTER 5
JANE SAYS—JANE'S ADDICTION

Oh, isn't that happy? That's sweet. Good for Judy. She's in her little blue chair. All wrapped up in a nice pretty little bow. That's a cute way to end the little story.

Yeah, sarcasm and dry wit come in real handy when you're on the journey to find the answer to the profound life question "Why am I so fucked up and how do I become not-so-fucked up?"

No, finding my blue chair was just the first step in what would be a two-year process.

Let's see. I had conquered the drinking problem—check. I had stayed on my medicine—check. Next in line on the To Do List in Life: Figure out why I kept screwing up the relationships in my life and what the hell was wrong with me.

Isn't it funny how music and relationships go hand in hand? For me love is always tied to music.

I remember my first radio and cassette player. It signified my entrance into the world of boy-girl relationships. I think I was probably 14 years old. The sounds of Air Supply filled the house, with me singing how I was "all out of love and so lost with it." (For those of you who are not hip as to Air Supply's coolness—That's a song title).

Oh how I wanted to be in love. I wanted to be "making love out of nothing at all" even though I had no idea what the song meant. But whatever it meant, it sounded wonderful!!! There I was, 14 years old, dancing around the room in my headphones, longing for love and dreaming about how wonderful it would be when I finally found it.

I mean, love had to be wonderful, right? All these songs say it is, so it must be. Oh what I wouldn't give to have someone love me like that! "Here I AMMMMMMMMMMMMMMM… the one that you love…asking for another dayyyyyyyyyyyyyyyyyyyyyyyy."

I learned everything there was to learn about relationships and sex from music. Let me tell you how pissed I was when I found out that Rick Springfield had gotten married! I ripped that poster off my closet door, I cried for hours on end! He was dead to me. Dead to me, I said! I loved him. I loved him truly, madly and a mite bit insanely as any preteen loves the pop star on the cover of Tiger Beat Magazine.

Oh, I got over him. Don't you worry—I moved on to the next greatest thing to ever hit the soil of the United States: Duran Duran. Oh yeah, baby! Simon LeBon—mmm…mmm…good! Now, Nick Taylor, he had a little too much make-up for my taste. But John Taylor—whew!!!!!! That guy was hot. And yes, I do still remember the drummer's name…Roger! Sigh! Oh, sweet, delicious, silent Roger, my little drummer boy. I will walk to the beat of your drum, yes I will.

The Duran Duran poster took over the spot that was previously occupied by that bastard, Rick Springfield.

The aching moans and groans in the song "Hungry Like the Wolf" – that was sex. Pure, raw, hot, animalistic, steamy sex: that is what those sounds meant! That was what good sex was supposed to sound like! I mean, if Simon LeBon could elicit moans and groans like that, that was the kind of sex I wanted to have!!!!

Thank God for the birth of Friday Night Videos! My parents wouldn't get MTV, but don't think that stopped me! I would stay up all night to catch Friday Night Videos at midnight. There was the pure hot yumminess of the video for "The Reflex," "Save a Prayer," and of course, "Rio." All of these provided delightfully sexy visual aides to the preteen who had no clue about boys, kissing and dating.

As you read before, I was a very, very late bloomer. There were no hot make-out parties for little Judy. No games of spin the bottle or seven minutes in heaven. No boys really seemed to be interested in the geeky little girl with braces, coke-bottle glasses and clothes from the Sears catalog.

All I knew was that love was wonderful according to all the songs on the radio, and I didn't have it and I wanted it. Badly.

The place was Adams Middle School. I was standing around lost in my dreams that the hot boy in 9th grade, Scott Something or Other, would come ask me to dance and of course it was to the most romantic song of all times. "Crazy For You," by Madonna. Oh, how he would hold me close and we would gaze into each other's eyes and he would think that I was the most amazing thing that had ever walked the face of the earth.

Coming out of my daydream, I saw him walking towards me. Towards me!!!! Yeah, right, like that would actually happen. He kept walking and asked some cheerleader to dance. Oh well, at least I had my dreams.

And dreams were about all I had. Let me tell you. I lived in a world of musical daydreams for a long, long, long time!

Middle school became high school, Madonna became Billy Idol and I stayed the same. Same daydreams, same fantasies. I would lie in bed at night and create these very elaborate movie scripts about the geeky girl who turns into the beautiful swan and the boy of her dreams, who she has admired from afar, falls in love with her and they live happily ever after.

Pathetic, huh? God, I hated high school. I hated that stupid little insipid girl who gawked at the football players and dreamed that one day she would be walking the hall wearing Jay Gruden's football jacket. Oh, how I dreamed of wearing that number 7. I had the biggest crush on him in 1985. Ask him, Jay will tell you. It really was pathetic. But as pitiful as it was, did I let the fact that he was the star quarterback and a senior stop me, the stupid, geeky little sophomore, from talking to him?

Oh, hell no! I marched my little butt right up to him and asked him to the Sadie Hawkins dance. Did he say yes? No. Of course not. But at least he was sweet about it and we sort of became friends after that.

But see, that little bit of rejection did not stop me from chasing my dreams! And that is what is important. I have a saying that goes like this: "The Bliss of Ignorance trumps the Fear of Failure every time!" I am so blissfully ignorant in so many ways!!!

Here is a little added note to that story—he was all kinds of wanting me when he saw me at a country bar many years later. He told me with a very big smile that I had grown up. Wink,

wink—I was wearing incredibly tight jeans and a very, very flattering top. Laughing, I just smiled and said, "See what you missed out on?"

So, yeah—in the end the ugly ducking became a beautiful swan. The quarterback got married, had some kids and I have no idea what he is doing now. As for the swan, she was about to learn a very painful lesson in life.

Love is not as wonderful as Air Supply made it out to be. In fact, for me it was more like a Jane's Addiction song.

In the lyrics to the song "Jane Says" by Jane's Addiction, the character Jane states she's never been in love, and she doesn't know what love is. She only knows if someone wants her.

That is how I summed up my life. When I became the swan, I didn't think of myself as a swan. I wasn't beautiful inside. Inside I was the same little girl I'd always been. Inside I had braces and coke-bottle glasses; I was a chubby, self-hating, needy, insecure little girl who just wanted a boy to love her.

But I wasn't a little girl anymore. I was a woman. I was 5'6, 120 pounds with boobs the size of watermelons. I got a lot of attention. But I didn't know how to deal with it or what to do with it. I was completely unprepared for life, love and relationships.

Hence the fact that I screwed up everything I touched. I screwed every man I touched and I screwed over my girlfriends with my touch of death.

I was Jane. All I knew was that I only knew when someone wanted me. It was the only thing I was sure of when it came to love and relationships. I described it in therapy as the Barbie doll syndrome.

I was the Barbie doll that sat on the shelf. Guys would take me down and play with me, because I was tons of fun. I drank and partied, I cussed up a storm, I was always available for a midnight booty call – but then it always came time when the guy would decide that Barbie wasn't fun anymore and she had to be put back on the shelf.

During graduate school I figured I would kill two birds with one stone. I focused on women's development. That way I could get credit for actually trying to fix myself. There is actually a lot of information in the area of women's development regarding the theory of "wanting to be wanted." Polly Young Eisendrath wrote several books on this topic and boy does she have it right. I am going to digress a minute here to give you some insight into this little theory.

Young-Eisendrath shows how women become the object of desire under control of the subject, which is the master. She answers the age -old question, "What do women want?" with the statement that what women want is to be wanted. She states that this is ultimately harmful to women. It puts women in the role of object versus being the subject of their own lives. Being an object of desire removes the self from the person; there is no core self, no clear autonomy and no self-determination. The woman's life becomes determined in relation to the man that is the subject in the relationship.

In seeking validation and approval of others, women gradually lose sight of themselves, their desires, their needs, wants and wishes. Ultimately, women become Objects of Desire and start to see themselves from a third person point of view. Young-Eisendrath shows that this leads to doubt of the self (abilities and knowledge). This leads to the need for reassurance and flattery from others. "Unable to know ourselves authentically, we want to be wanted instead of loved."

She states that while women lose track of being able to control their own lives, this feels normal because every other woman is doing it and it has been this way for so long.

Women are taught from an early age that in order to feel complete, there must be validation from others. Women are entranced with the idea of "wanting to be wanted" and confuse the desire of being wanted with being loved. Society is bombarded through magazines, videos, TV and movies with the images of the beautiful muse. Young-Eisendrath describes how men and women alike worship the muse. The muse is the young, stunning girl who represents all things beautiful, nice, self-sacrificing, etc...the muse is the maiden in fairy tales with no power of her own, i.e. Cinderella, Snow White. In contrast, the "hag-bitch" is the opposite of the muse and unfortunately, married women turn into the hag-bitch. It is celebrated to be the bride but it is never celebrated to be the wife.

Hmmm. A little something to noodle on there, huh? Well, when I discovered this information, I ran out and bought every book she wrote and absorbed all she had to say. I could relate. Well, with this information from Polly's years of academic research, it all made sense to me! Wanting to be wanted. That was me. Readers, think about it for a moment. Wanting to be wanted. Flattery, attention, looks, a man desiring you.

So what would happen when the man didn't want me anymore? I would find the next one who would. I always defined myself in relation to the man I was with at the time. After all this time, in my mid-thirties I still didn't know what love was. I only knew when someone wanted me.

It validated my existence. However, life as the Barbie doll sitting on that shelf was a lonely existence. It was a never-ending cycle of depression, self-hatred, self-destruction and thoughts of suicide.

I can always associate every painful relationship moment with a song. They were entwined with pieces of my heart and the salt of my tears.

Lone Justice—"Shelter"

My 20th birthday party. Kemy Aznabay had broken my heart. I put in my cassette of the single "Shelter" by Lone Justice. It played over and over and over. All I remember are the lights from the equalizer and the pain I felt. Sobbing to the lyrics, I passed out alone on my living room floor from all the alcohol and pot in my system.

Bonnie Raitt—"I Can't Make You Love Me"

Slow dancing at Pleasure Island with Michael Strickland and trying so hard to make him love me. Two months later sitting in my little red CRX drunk and crying my eyes out in front of his apartment because I finally faced the fact that he didn't love me and would never love me.

U.R.O.K.—"Sea Green Eyes"

On stage with the band at Kasey's Kove, nothing but a drunk Judy, the guitar, Greg and one pissed-off girlfriend getting ready to kick my ass.

Garth Brooks—"Shameless"

Drunk and sobbing because Brian Ziegler just wanted to be friends. I pulled over on some rural road because I was trying to find a telephone pole to run into.

Roger from The Sharks, Dave from U.R.O.K., Scott from Baylife, Ari, Yasser, Cris Boyar, Brian from Despoparados, Roger from American Cowboy, some guy, some song—and it always ended the same.

Me—being incredibly needy, love me, love me, smothering, smothering. Me—having sex to get love. Me—just so desperately wanting to be loved.

Why was I so alone? Why was I so horrible that no one would ever love me? What was wrong with me? I hated myself, I hated the world, I hated everything. I hated everything and I wanted the pain to stop.

On October 18, 1996 I thought my pain would stop. I got married. I had a man that loved me beyond belief. But it didn't stop, it got worse. Now I was not just hurting myself; there was another important human being involved.

The vortex of my own self-destruction was spinning faster and faster. It was sucking more than just me into it. It had destroyed my first marriage, my relationship with several close friends, my in-laws and my own parents. Soon it would suck my second husband, my beloved young adult step sons and more loved ones.

My self-destructiveness, my dirty little secret that I ran and hid from all these years, my own little circle of death kept going round and round. Damn it if God was not going to let me off that easy. The fact of the matter was that taking away the depressants like alcohol only got me to the fifty-yard line.

So, there I was in therapy, summer of 2004. Sober. Medicated. Single. My new therapist, Tom Watkins, was my substance abuse counselor and luckily for me, he happened to be a relationship counselor as well. Apparently, according to Tom, all this mess was all tied together anyway. I credit much of my success to Tom. He is a great therapist, very subtle, but always right on target. We have very good discussions and I always feel like I am making progress when I walk out of the door.

After the separation from my second husband, I put myself on a mandatory man sabbatical. The biggest plus of this little furlough was that if I did not interact with men I was safe. Safe and secure. No heartache, no screwing things up, no hurting others, no more collateral damage.

Safe and secure. Safe in my little cocoon. Just me and my music. Who needs men anyway, I would say. I'm done with them all! I am obviously not good at relationships as history as shown us. So I will just hide away. Safe and secure. The world is a safer place now. My world was a safer place.

The longer I hid in my little cocoon, my nest, my haven, the longer I put off actually having to deal with men. You know, maybe what I needed was some relationship education. I was obviously very big on self-analysis and whatnot. So, I could probably learn a lot about why I was so messed up by educating myself.

So I began to gather all the required reading materials for Relationships 101. Now, since I could not actually find an accredited, legitimate place that offered some type of degree program in Real Life & Relationships, I figured I would research it on my own. Self-directed study, if you will. Then, once I had learned the "technical" aspects of relationships, I would venture out (slowly, in a safe atmosphere) to conduct some sociological experiments with the necessary data population, i.e. men. Once I had sufficiently mastered that, I would move into Advanced Life Prep. This would entail actual "hands on interaction" (insert cheesy porn music here…bomchickabombom).

I felt it would be best if I started at the beginning, going on the assumption that everything that I knew about relationships was inaccurate.

Now, I am going to take a few moments to point out some interesting things I learned in my research. Then I will get back to why I still think good music is better than sex. I want to share this with my dear Readers because frankly, it's cheaper than you all going to therapy, I don't want to be a knowledge hoarder and lastly, because I wrote some really funny little stories.

So just go with the flow with me on this. Here is a little bit of what I have learned in my Journey de Relationships.

CHAPTER 6
THE TROUBLE WITH LOVE IS—KELLY CLARKSON
Profound Insight #1

The majority of problems we adults seem to complain about in regard to relationships are probably because we have no clue as to what the hell we are doing, why we are doing it or how to fix it.

Did you know that relationships had stages? Seriously, did you guys know that? I mean, if you did I feel like a total dumbass. But this article that I stumbled across really was an eye opener. Huh. I did not know this information. I found this article called "The Stages of Committed Relationships" on www.relationship-institute.com.

There are six stages of committed relationships:

- **The romantic phase** (the Hollywoodized version of love—you know, the honeymoon phase, all lovey dovey, flowers, love poems, romance out the wazhoo, "we're so in love"!!!!) My friends and I would call this the "Dreamweaver" stage—like the song Dreamweaver by Gary Wright...Oooh, ooh dreamweaver, I believe we can make it through the niiiiiii iiiiiiiighhhhhhhhhhhhttttttttt. Everytime Laura would be around this one guy, it was like she was in a trance, just gazing at him and sighing those deep sighs of lust. Then we would surround her and start singing "Dreamweaver, I believe we can make it through the niiiiiiiiiiiiiiighhhhhhhhhhhhhhhhhhhhhhtt." If she were a cartoon character, little stars would be shooting out her eyes and the red heart would start thumping. Get the idea?
- **The adjusting to reality stage** (the broken rose-colored glasses phase). This is where reality hits. I mean really, it is just not sexy for the man to be farting in the bed!!!! Plus, he is going to hear me go to the bathroom at some point in time. There is only so long you can avoid these things. The human factor of relationships... see this is where I always freaked out and took a hike. We women and our crazy ideas about relationships!! There is more to come on this topic. Why is it not romantic anymore? What happened to my idealistic Prince and who is this human fallible man?
- **The power struggle.** My views on relationships collide with his views. But mine are right. Right? Yeah? No, no my ideas are not even in the ballpark of reality. Okay, maybe not even in the same state as the ballpark.
- **The re-evaluation phase** This would be where the word "commitment" comes into the phrase "committed relationships." See, me—I had no comprehension of commitment. No clue what it took to really make a relationship work. I just tossed each relationship out when it didn't live up to my expectations.
- **Reconciliation** Actually working through the problems versus running away like me.
- And then finally, **acceptance.**

It's a roadmap to successful relationships, if you will. Apparently we all go through the same stages. Everyone, meaning all races, all religions, all sexual orientations…you get the picture. We all experience the same feelings, give or take.

Why is the divorce rate so high? I don't have a hard scientific answer to this, but for me I know that I had completely unrealistic ideas and beliefs on how marriage and committed relationships worked. I had no idea what kind of hard work it took. My marriages may have gotten to stage 3, but I was stuck in stage 1.

Where do these insane and unrealistic ideas about love and marriage come from? Well, it starts with fairy tales and ends with Lifetime Movie Channel. So, I decided to rewrite a classic fairy tale.

Cinderella

Let's delve into the "behind the scenes" that was left out…What really happens to Cinderella after Prince C. sticks her shoe back on her foot?

My guess is this: they date and have sex about ten times a week, always in the morning, plus secret little breaks from work for a quickie around lunchtime, and then they get engaged. They have a full on-off-the-hook party at the castle for the wedding and reception.

After the honeymoon, they come back and set up house in the mini-castle down the road from the in-laws. Sex starts to decline to about three times a week, then twice, then every Friday. Prince C starts bitching about the lack of sex, Cindy starts complaining that he never listens to her and never does anything romantic anymore. She gets pregnant, gains about 40 pounds.

Prince C starts playing golf every weekend while Cindy redecorates the mini-castle. She has the baby and they name her Snow Charming, after Cindy's best friend. Cindy has postpartum depression.

Prince C has built a "workshop" out back that really holds a large screen plasma TV, PS 2, Xbox 360, all the Vice City games, a computer with a web cam, a foosball table, a large cooler filled with beer, and a microwave. Prince C gains an extra 30 pounds from the beer.

Cindy cries all the time, baby Snow cries all the time and the fights have stopped. Now they just don't talk anymore.

Several years down the road and two more kids later, Cindy finds out that Prince C has been sleeping with Snow White for the past year. Then, in the screaming and yelling, it comes out that Cindy has been having an on-line affair with a guy in the neighboring village. Cindy says to hell with this, takes off and goes to live with the guy in the neighboring village. He says (according to his fairytalematchmaker.com profile) that he is a good listener, enjoys talking about his feelings while taking long walks on the beach and loves nothing more than to cuddle with his soul mate for hours on end.

That is the real story behind the fairy tale.

The Grand Gesture:

Where else do we women get these stupid ideas about love and relationships? How about the Grand Gesture, hmmm? Now, c'mon Readers, don't pretend like ya'll don't know what I am talking about.

Men, if you are reading this, first off –thank you, I'm flattered. Secondly, you are about to learn a piece of wisdom that has eluded the male species for as long as humans have walked the earth. The Grand Gesture probably has never been explained to the male population prior to this. It is a secret that even women are embarrassed to talk about openly. But if you pay close attention to conversations amongst the female tribe, you may be able to pick up little tidbits or subtle hints of this evasive mythical beast.

Here it is. The Grand Gesture is a tool of measurement. It is the scale by which all women measure the level of her man's attentiveness, then love, and from thereon after, his level of commitment. This scale is not in writing, it is not embedded in stone. It is a secret that is passed down from generation to generation. It is an unspoken cultural more that I am fairly sure can only be found in female human beings.

For the visual types of readers, I am including specific examples of what can be considered Grand Gestures. These will help the male readers understand what it is, how it works and how to be successful in delivering the Grand Gesture.

- **Say Anything**: A movie from the late 80s. I think this was one of Cameron Crowe's first films. The scene that embodies the Grand Gesture is as follows: John Cusack is standing outside the girl's window playing "In Your Eyes" by Peter Gabriel very loudly with the boom box held high above his head. This action is to proclaim his affection for the young lady and announce to the entire neighborhood that he likes her. It is not necessarily for her, that is a byproduct. It is really to announce to the world that he likes her. That scene really is the bomb and kudos to Cameron Crowe's wife, ex -Heart singer/guitarist Nancy Wilson, for coming up with the idea of using that song. Bravo. (How cheesy is this? I still think that really would be awesome, and yet, at 36, I still dream of it. At least I admit it).

- **Pretty Woman**: The film from the 80's, which is completely hokey and really very socially irresponsible. I mean, it gives all those crack-whore prostitutes the false hope that some hottie millionaire is going to actually fall in love with them. Nonetheless, the Grand Gesture occurs when Richard Gere drives up in a limo with flowers, screaming to the world that he loves Vivian (Julia Roberts), his hooker girlfriend. Okay, first of all, there is how unrealistic this shit is, how irresponsible Hollywood is, and last but not least, what suckers the American public really are. It doesn't matter that the chick is a whore, a whore by the true definition of taking money for sexual services, not even some high-class call girl. A whore, standing on a street corner in seedy LA. Her choice of life profession is not relevant. It is not even relevant that she needs an HIV test as well as a trip to the lawyer's office to sign the pre-nup. Just because she won't kiss him on the mouth doesn't mean she hasn't had sex for money with about 300 guys before him. Niiiiiiiice. What *is* relevant is this: the loud proclamation once again to the entire neighborhood of that low-income crime-infested area where all Vivian's friends and relatives congregate. Loud proclamation. Loud proclamation of love to all the people who are meaningful to the female's life. Loud.

- **Jerry McGuire**: Yet another movie, this time in the 1990's. First, let me preface: I cannot stand Tom Cruise. I detest Tom Cruise. That is another story. What is relevant from this movie is this: Jerry comes into the room of Renee Zellweger's house, which happens to be filled with women who hate him for dumping the girl. These women hate him, he broke their friend's heart, and he ruined her life. She quit her job to follow him, married his sorry ass even though it was very obvious that he was not ready for the whole thing. And here it is…he overcomes all the bad things he did…by what? A proclamation of love to her, and more importantly, all her friends who hate his guts. We women, we are really pathetic. And frankly not that hard to figure out. Pathetic. I'm ashamed to be a woman.

- **An Officer and A Gentleman**: Another movie with Richard Gere…mmm…yummy. Even more yummy in uniform. This is getting predictable, isn't it? He dumped her, broke her heart and left a bunch of factory workers ready to kill him. However, in true Grand Gesture fashion, he wins her back with the grandest gesture of all. Striding through that dirty, nasty paper factory, looking oh so gallant in his uniform and most certainly delicious, Mr. Gere sweeps Debra Winger off her feet and carries her out of that putrid hellhole of an existence. And all of her friends look on in envy, yet clapping loudly for the Grand Gesture, because secretly they know that if it can happen to Debra Winger, it can happen for them. And…yes…I do still dream of a hot guy in uniform sweeping me off my feet from the factory that I don't work in…Ahhhh…perhaps one day. As he carries me away, I smile and say aloud, "How ya like me now, bitches???" And that, my dear male readers…is what it is all about.

CHAPTER 7
DREAMS—KENNY CHESNEY

Picture this: I'm driving down the road, listening to the Chesney CD *No Shirt, No Shoes, No Problem*. It's good, but you know, it is just background music while I am thinking about my life, wondering if I am really ever actually going to find Mr. Long Term Meaningful Committed Relationship That Will Not End in Divorce. I was pretty down in the dumps. I'm having a little pity party with myself, wallowing in my blues, feeling as if I am doomed to walk this earth alone in never-ending aloneness. I'm depressed and frustrated with my history of heartache.

Then here comes this song. Track number 8. It is an "Oh. My. God" moment.

How could someone take exactly, word for word, what had been on my mind at that exact particular minute and put it into song? Especially some guy from Tennessee who lives on a beach, hanging out all day in some blue chair. A guy, a man, a male specimen, he of the male gender— how the hell can he say what I was thinking?

Now look, I don't mean he knew the emotion I was feeling and put it into song. No. I mean word for freaking word. I literally pulled the car over and sat and listened with my mouth open. What the hell? Was this some freaky sign from God? Have you ever read *The Celestine Prophecy*? This was one of those Celestine moments.

"Surreal" is the only word to best describe the moment, surreal and freaking scary.

Dreams—Kenny Chesney

She says most men her age want younger women
She thinks her self-esteem is not quite itself anymore
But she sees herself as more than what the mirror shows
And why that's so important heaven only knows
When the important part
For her is souls and hearts and
Dreams, sharing a life and a home
Dreams, of never ever being alone again
Not even diamonds just a little gold
Someone there to hold her hand when she gets old
Dreams, the kind you know will never end
Forever lovers and forever friends
Someone really there to love and care and share
Dreams
She swears she won't divorce a third time
She swears the more she knows about love
The harder it is to find
The perfect picture of her white horse prince
Is now dependability and common sense
Someone kind and brave
Someone not afraid of
Dreams, the kind you know will never end
Forever lovers and forever friends
Someone really there to love and care and share
Dreams
She says most men her age want younger women

I sat there on the side of the road, staring at my CD player in a freaked-out trance. Here's the punch line. Just that morning, standing in the hallway in my office, I had said the following: "I refuse to get divorced for a third time. I don't believe all that fairy tale stuff anymore, I know it's not real. I have had the big diamond; I just want a simple band. I want that true intimacy that comes from a foundation that only a deep friendship, a deep commitment and sharing of common dreams can bring. I don't want to divorce a third time."

Wow. Pretty freaky, huh? I pulled out the CD jacket. It turns out that according to Chesney's little reflection that he writes about each song, he wrote this after his mother had called him because her boyfriend had just broken up with her and she said that the men her age want younger women.

First of all, bravo to Chesney for having written a song for his mom—now that is a grand gesture of love. Second, I want to call Mrs. Chesney up and talk to her. Don't I know exactly how she feels! And damn, I'm 36 now. Only 36. When the hell did I get to be 36 and when did the guys that I am interested in start wanting younger women???? When did I get old?

Some female readers may not have approached this life milestone yet. Personally, I wasn't ready for it. I was not at all prepared for the emotional turmoil I would experience. No one had warned me about this or the reaction that I would have. I never used to worry about age until recently.

All of a sudden, I wasn't the young hottie in the bar. It had been awhile since I'd been the young hottie in the bar; I'd been out of the dating game for over ten years. I'd been replaced by a younger, cuter, perkier, smaller version. Am I middle-aged now? Oh my God. I am middle-aged now.

I know you are sitting there reading, thinking, "Oh, but you're only 36, and that is still young." Well, I thought so too, but really it's true. I have just spent months dating and I found that men my age want younger women!!! What the hell?

You want evidence? Go on www.match.com and look at all the guys. Guys who are 39 are seeking women 18-40. 18???? What the hell is that all about? That is like me dating one of my stepson's friends. Gross. Now, I know that I have no room to speak because my second husband was 14 years older than me. But now I am on the opposite side of the fence. Ouch.

I'm looking in the age range of 32—39. But these guys aren't looking for me. They don't want the baggage that comes from women their own age. They want the young hot chicks that can be impressed by their worldliness and sophistication. The guys that I am attracted to don't want a twice-divorced, sober alcoholic doctoral student who runs a company, makes good money, and has a loud biological clock.

Now, guys a lot older than me are interested in me. I have guys that are in their late 50s emailing me. Trust me, I have heard it all! You wouldn't believe the emails. "Let me treat you like a princess, take you away from all your worries, take care of you, blah, blah, blah." I know that I want someone in my own age range for my own specific compatibility reasons.

Men my age want younger women. You know what, I completely agree with Mrs. Chesney. The more I know about love, the harder it is to find. Now that I know what I want, I won't settle for less. It is extremely depressing and frustrating.

I mean, think about it. Should I settle for less just because I don't want to be alone? No. Of course not. It's funny, because I have gotten to the point in my life where I will evaluate a possible date and think...hmmm...meet someone new, do the small talk chit chat nonsense, go through the motions, smile and nod, smile and nod OR chill out at home with my good friend and back-up singer, Kenneth A. Chesney? Hmm...some people would think that is a tough choice. Not me. I choose Chesney every time.

Why? Because I know how it ends. And the Chesney choice always ends happily.

CHAPTER 8
WHAT'S LOVE GOT TO DO WITH IT—TINA TURNER

When I was little I did not sit around dreaming of the day my second set of divorce papers would lay in front of me.

No, I dreamed of my wedding day. I dreamed of all eyes on me, how beautiful I looked, how envious every female was when they cast their eyes upon my glory. In these dreams, I think that I was probably 30 pounds lighter and I looked amazing. In my own mind, I was the vision of beauty, something airbrushed out of a Glamour Shots photo, yet not in some cheesy outfit with a fake "realtor" smile plastered on my face. Me. Only Better.

My dreams did not include thoughts of a second divorce. Thoughts such as, "Oh shit; here I go again," "What a fucking loser," and the ever-present "Twice divorced—unfuckingbelievable."

The positive things about choosing good music over sex are: 1) It is cheaper than dating 2) It does not come with sexually transmitted diseases, unless you are some nasty-ass groupie sucking on Scott Stapp and Kid Rock's you-know-what appendage—GROSS! 3) You don't have to worry about that awkward morning-after situation. 4) Chris Cagle will call me back and I will see him again, because all I have to do is press play to see his video on my iPod, damn it. 5) I have already screened out those I like and don't like, therefore I don't have to waste time pretending to like those that I really don't like, and if I really like you, i.e. Gary Allan, you are upgraded to full playlist status. 6) Kenny Chesney does not require me to spend hours rehashing every instant message, email, and conversation using the mental instant replay feature to analyze every minute of every minute that I spent with the jackass that walked out of my door after four months of dating. Who ultimately will resurface after five months of no contact only to not give me an explanation and just pretend that nothing happened. Nope, Kenny just sings to me and doesn't screw with my mind. I know right where I stand with him. Lastly, and most importantly: 7) It gives me a helluva lot of time to think.

God, I do a lot of thinking, don't I? Sometimes, even I have a hard time being me. It's very exhausting sometimes.

But, anyhoo. I have done quite a bit of thinking. I have thunk, I have done all of the following: assess, evaluate, examine, inspect, investigate, scrutinize, arrange, assort, catalog (*or* catalogue), categorize, classify, codify, diagram, index, order, schematize, sort, tabulate, divide, reduce, segment, separate, subdivide. Thank you, dictionary.com! Here are my thoughts, theories and ideas on the whole dating and marriage situation.

The fact of the matter is this. While at first love is all gooey, mushy, butterflies, hot intense pangs of anticipation of impending sex, then lots of hot intense sex, feelings of pain and torment in which it feels like your heart is being physically removed from your chest when the phone doesn't ring...this all goes away.

Some time, somewhere, somehow, all those passionate, overwhelming feelings will dissipate.

Dissipate, like water drops on a hot black asphalt road in July in Texas in a record-breaking heat wave. *Te comprende?*

Practicality of love isn't very romantic. It isn't very sexy and it isn't very glamorous. But it is a fact of life. There are so many shades of love. I have now decided that if I combine the chemistry and passion of feelings with the practical nature of a business merger, I will have the formula for a successful, long-term, meaningful, committed relationship that will not end in divorce.

I have experienced a lot of success in my professional life. Maybe if I applied what I had learned in my professional life to my personal life, I could have the same success.

What do I mean by practical nature of a business merger? When you enter into a business relationship with another person, typically you form some type of partnership (i.e. limited partnership, limited liability company, that type of thing). Upon doing this, your lawyer comes up with the draft operating agreement or partnership agreement. Then both parties, via their lawyers, negotiate the business points.

Everything in life is negotiable. Every situation can be a win-win for all involved. It just takes patience, skill and good, open communication.

Hmm…yes this does sound like a pre-nuptial agreement, and here is why I am now a proponent of them. First off, there is a template document that outlines the responsibilities of the partnership/"family" – what are the goals, what is the purpose, what is our mission? These are all put in writing. Perhaps the mission of my future family is to have four children. My mate only wants one. We either negotiate for a win-win, or we walk away because we have incompatible goals. Obviously, I will not marry someone who doesn't like children. Incompatible goals. No matter how hot he is or how good he is in bed. Really, really, really good in bed, and beautiful with a body like Adonis, and literally makes me drool, it doesn't matter because we have incompatible goals for our family.

Second, what is a "deal-killer"? What would kill the partnership? Stealing money from the company, trading secrets, conflict of interest—in a business those are avoided by legal remedies. So, what happens when one person wants out because he or she is mad at the other? See, this is a good time to discuss this type of thing. What is a deal-killer? Adultery, drug dealing, sociopathic serial killing? These shades of grey need to be outlined so that all parties are on the same page.

For instance, in my third marriage/partnership documents, I think that I could get over a one-night stand. Frankly, I don't think I would want to know about it. It would be hard to work through, but that would not be a deal-killer for me.

What about murder? Okay, well, off the cuff, my readers would probably say, definitely a deal killer. But what if my husband was driving and was in an accident and killed the other driver? Negligent homicide. Would I leave? No, bad times are bad times. That is the test of a true, strong relationship. Remember Stage 4?

I have to run through these scenarios and ask myself, "Am I committed to the long term nature of this relationship?" Serial killer, pedophile… well damn, I would hope that my screening process is a little more intensive and would weed the sociopaths out.

Third, what really does happen when one party seriously wants to leave? In my partnership agreement it will include the following: Should one party desire to separate and terminate the marital union, the following must occur: a) no involvement of any third party for either primary party during the separation b) mandatory marital counseling as well as individual counseling for a minimum of six months and c) arbitration and mediation.

Now, Readers, you are probably thinking that such a formal and professional business-like approach is not very sexy and romantic. Well, neither is divorce, and as I have mentioned, I am not getting divorced a third time.

So, my future familial partnership agreement will be in place to ensure that there are no miscommunications, no misunderstandings and a clear understanding of the path this family is following. It will be in place to ensure that there is no third divorce for Judy M. Core. Mrs. Chesney and I are in staunch agreement in that matter. No more divorce.

Remember a few paragraphs ago I said that I had learned a lot from my professional life? Well, here is the most important thing I learned: "loyalty" and "trust" are just words until you sign your name on the dotted line of a legal document.

See, lots of people can talk a big game, but if you can't sign your name on the bottom line and put a dog in the fight next to my dog, then shut the hell up. Loyalty is just a word. Trust is just a word. Put up or shut up.

Trust me, at the end of the day in a legal dispute, divorce, business litigation, whatever it is it, always ends up being every man or woman for himself or herself. So why go into a relationship with a rose-colored view of happily ever after thinking that you are never going to have troubles? I have done this, twice. It didn't work out all that well. Shouldn't we plan for the worst case scenario ahead of time?

We do in business. No one would invest in your company if you did not have contingency plans, succession plans and exit strategies.

What happens when one party wants to leave, and violates the above stated terms? Financial penalty and perhaps limited child visitation. Okay, well, definitely financial penalty, because you have to have some dog in the fight in order to stay in the marriage. Each party, by the way, not just the man.

I do not understand this situation here. How is it, that if a woman cheats on her husband and leaves him, and he did not want to end the marriage, he has to support her financially? By the way, this woman is not me, but this is a real situation. It is a guy that I dated for a little while and his ex-wife. She should have kept her ass at home but he is the one that has to pay, literally. That is just messed up.

Everything should be fair and equitable. Win-win, remember? Everything in life is negotiable.

Now, personally, I don't believe in the overall theory of alimony. Yes, I believe in child support. I do believe that if I am going to give up my livelihood of financial independence to enter into this union then should my mate violate the above stated terms…that boy's gonna pay me a yearly sum equal to what I currently make plus 10% for each year of the marriage for a minimum of five years.

What, what, what? Yeah, you heard me. Look kids, I am a partner in a company. I make good money. I have the potential to make a lot more over the next fifteen years. Financial security means a lot. Should I just toss that out the door for some hot guy I just met six months ago and let him sweep me away to his tropical paradise, only to dump me for the 22-year-old nanny? Oh, hell no.

Fair and equitable. Loyalty and trust. Put up or shut up.

Think about it, if I commit an act of adulterly and will lose the previously agreed upon financial penalty of $500,000 in addition to divorce because of that act…guess what? A moment of heat in the sheets doesn't sound all that appealing anymore. The guy may have a body like Adonis, but is he worth $500,000? Mmm…maybe not so much.

See that is not so bad, is it? But it sure does make a lot of sense to negotiate this type of stuff ahead of time, right? Okay, calm down and just think rationally for a second. Doesn't it seem to make good sense to have it all out in the open so that decisions are not made out of emotions in the heat of bad times? Make the decisions ahead of time, let all the players know the rules, write them down and sign the papers.

Bad times, remember those? Bad times are the true test. Good times are just that, good times. Good times can be had by all, but good times are a dime a dozen.

The person who sticks by you in bad times, that person is golden. The person who says to you, "You know what? I don't understand you, but damn it if I don't still love you," that person is a keeper. By the way, Readers, that is a true statement. My best friend Jen Lawton McCaslin said that to me many years ago during a bad time. She is a keeper, and we've been best friends for more than ten years even though we are states apart.

CHAPTER 9
NO MORE DRAMA—MARY J. BLIGE

The high of the feelings, those gooey mushy feelings and pangs of hot lust in the beginning of the romance! Aren't they wonderful?

People can be addicted to the sensation of the high of drinking, the high of drugs, the high of risk-taking behavior, the rush of stealing. The overwhelming surge of hormones generated by these events can create a toxicity of addiction. So why can't a person be addicted to falling in love?

I definitely think that I was addicted to falling in love. The power of the first few months of dating…remember how those inevitable, crazy, indefinable love-like feelings invaded your mind and overrode your every thought and action? Do you recall that wave of ecstasy and excitement when you found out the guy you liked liked you, those feelings of connecting with someone else?

How many times have you said the following: "I've never felt this way before"? Maybe you said, "He makes me feel so alive." "He makes me feel like I am the most important thing in the world." "He gets me." "He understands me in a way that no one else ever has, I can feel it." "The chemistry between us is overwhelming, it is like an undercurrent of passion." What about, "It is like when we come together, there is something more powerful than us, we just feel so in sync with each other."

Isn't it funny that no matter how many relationships we go through, these same recurring feelings always take us by surprise? Like they are exclusive to that particular pairing of you and your beloved. It wasn't until a therapist pointed out that I had said those exact statements about several men that I saw the pattern. It was one of those moments where I did not receive the message very well. Sometimes it takes a while to see what is right in front of your face. I call it Inner Blindness.

Here is something that may surprise you—I used to make my decisions solely based on how I felt at the time. (*That is me being facetious*). My life was ruled by my heart. All my decisions, reactions and beliefs were based on my emotions and feelings at that particular time.

Sometimes my feelings didn't change for months or years. Sometimes they changed minute by minute. My life was in a constant state of flux.

If my feelings changed, I interpreted that as a message for me to make a change. I mistakenly believed that my feelings were the same thing as my intuition.

Those Other people who are pragmatic and level-headed, they just didn't get it. They couldn't hear the sounds of passion and emotion that the deeply hypersensitive artistic creative people hear. Those Other people were ruled by their heads. How boring. How unimaginative. How dull.

We creative passionate souls live with our hearts on our sleeves. We live deeply, love deeply and feel the highs of life as well as the excruciating depths of the lows with a sense of surrender. We are blessed, we are gifted. Those Other people are just wasting space on our blessed earth.

Looking back, I am fairly certain that I had put this belief in place to make me feel special about myself. The much-needed protection of the delicate little fragile self-esteem.

After much therapy and a post-medicated life, I saw and understood that people actually have happy fulfilling lives without being in a constant state of motion sickness from being on a mood/feeling/emotion roller coaster every day of their lives.

It doesn't have to be head versus heart, or heart versus head versus heated loins, for that matter—heated loins versus the tag team duo of heart and head! There actually can be a full integration and a happy co-existence of all three. And...the beauty of it all is that when all three (heart, head, heated loins) are in alignment, the outcomes, the results, the consequences of one's actions are SO MUCH BETTER.

No drama. Plain and simple. No fucking drama. Yes, regular life occurrences, regular life events, life, death, etc...BUT NO ADDITIONAL DRAMA!

So this is how the other half lives...amazing. Interesting and yes, amazing. Wow.

Here is a funny little side story. You know how we have that phrase "Can't see the forest for the trees"? That is that Inner Blindness thing. Well, prior to separation #2, I started seeing Dr. Alexander, the psychologist who got me out of the Pit of Despair. She asked me if I wanted to take this psychological test that would better help her help me. Furthermore, this would assist in my emotional development and self-growth.

So inside of me was a cocktail mix of a little bit of hesitation, a wee bit of fear but mostly a hefty dose of narcissistic anticipation of superior results. Oh yeah, I can laugh now! But then....

Holy shit. Holy, holy, holy shit. Yeah, the outcomes were that bad. Bad, bad, bad, very bad for me.

Let me educate you on how these tests work. Battery of questions of about 200, takes about an hour of time to complete. Then your "results" are basically a statistical scoring system that shows the psychologist if you have an Axis I diagnosis (brain disorder such as schizophrenia, bi-polar, schizoaffective, etc). Next it shows if you have a personality disorder.

I mean, really, there was no good news. Okay, well, I guess there is a little. I am not a sociopath. See, that is the optimism in me coming out!

So starting with the Axis I—I scored high enough to be diagnosed with Bi-Polar as well as Generalized Anxiety Disorder. Personality disorders showed the following traits, narcissism (egotistical), histrionic (drama queen), sadism (ass-kicker) and anti-social (defies authority and overall rule breaker). Well, hmmm, okay, not exactly what I was going for...a little something to noodle on there.

I was thinking more along the lines of "Emotionally well-developed, intellectually superior and overall well-balanced individual." Apparently, that would be the narcissism speaking!

I had a hard time swallowing the Bi-Polar part. From the time that I was about 23, the greatest, deepest, secret fear I held was that one day I would have my psychotic break and be hospitalized involuntarily. I would forever more be Mentally Ill. I would hear voices, have hallucinations, or maybe even be catatonic.

That again, is not one of those things that little girls sit and dream about. Can't you picture it? Little girls sitting around sharing their dreams…"I want to be a schizophrenic with audio hallucinations," "I want to be an alcoholic," "I want to be a crack whore," "No way, you guys, when I grow up I want to be a stripper, strung out on heroin, with an abusive boyfriend who beats the shit out of me!!!"

You get the picture.

Mental illness runs in my family and every day since I found out (at a Neil Diamond concert, from my sister) that my grandmother had been schizophrenic and hospitalized many, many times after many, many suicide attempts, I have worried about the day that it would strike me. Mental illness runs throughout my family tree, a little Bi-Polar on this limb, a dash of schizophrenia dangling from that branch, and of course with God's love for black comedy…I figured it was only a matter of time before it struck me.

Irony, oh sweet unbelievable irony. Do you get the irony? Me, the psychology major, the mental health case manager, the mental health counselor, forensic mental health liaison, me with the MA in Human Development…Me?

As it turns out, after much discussion with Dr. Alexander, it would appear that I probably am not a "true" Bi-Polar. I am Cyclothymiac. Which would be what? Well, as it turns out, it is something like a low-grade Bi-Polar. The swings aren't as drastic but I'm not even-keeled like people are supposed to be.

I have never had the massive swings between mania (the up-ness) and depression for weeks on end. I won't go into a long dialogue explaining the intricacies of the whole diagnosis but I will just tell you what I took from it.

Those close to me always have described me as moody, high-maintenance, emotional, needy, clingy one minute, reclusive and isolating the next, jumping in and out of relationships, making impulse purchases, etc. See now, I thought all females were this way. I'm serious!!!!

A lot of people debate the validity and science behind mental illnesses, but look, my opinion is that with the understanding of my limitations, my weaknesses, my "defects" or whatever the hell label you want to put on my problems with my moods and emotions, the diagnosis has, at a minimum, made me understand how to handle damage control in my life.

I know my triggers; I warn people if I haven't taken my medicine due to some foul up by the idiots at the CVS pharmacy. I always try to get enough sleep, I exercise and I don't drink. I track my moods and my emotions.

So…whew…with all that heavy stuff out of the way, I began to realize that my head, my heart and my heated loins could actually be in alignment. And it is so relieving when they are. It makes decision-making so much easier when it comes to relationships.

All that rambling for a new simple rule that I live by. Here it is:

Profound insight #2:

Unless all three parties: the Head, Heart and the Heated Loins, are all in agreement as to what consequent action should be taken…no action should be taken.

Pretty freaking simple, huh? I think so. This commandment of mine has increased the quality of my decision-making abilities a million times over. That, my dear readers, is an amazing ROI (return on investment).

CHAPTER 10
A MURDER OF ONE—COUNTING CROWS

"So, how ya doing? Yeah, I heard about your divorce. Hmm, yes the second divorce...well you know some people are just unlucky in love. Don't worry. I'm sure you'll find someone. There's someone for everyone. Are you dating again? Is it serious? Is he the One? Well, if it's meant to be, then it's meant to be. The Universe will bring you your soul mate when you are ready." ARGGGGGGGGGGGGGGG!

Ah, yes the dreaded small talk conversation with people I haven't seen in awhile. Then there are always the family gatherings on a yearly basis. "How you've been? What have you been up to? I heard you got married. Oh...mmm...divorced already. Well, that didn't last long now, did it?"

I am starting to think that my family members are thinking that I am a lesbian and they are just waiting patiently for me to come out of the closet. I mean, really, what else possibly could explain two divorces? They probably are standing around the sink washing dishes murmuring with deep sighs, "Yes, well it's only a matter of time before the big announcement hits. Yep, yep, we're pretty sure she's a lesbian. Well, for one, she is writing some book about music being better than sex, so that is one clue. Then there is the fact that when I ask her about dating, she says she is dating her iPod. She can't keep a man, so maybe she'll have more luck with women. Well, there goes the dream of a grandbaby any time soon."

Yeah, well, I'm not a lesbian. Sorry folks, there is no easy answer for two failed marriages.

People are always looking for an easy answer for things. Well, she must be a lesbian. Well, she obviously has incredibly bad karma and has pissed off Fate and Destiny. Well, she stopped going to church, if she would just get right with God, he'd bring her happiness. Destiny, Fate, Universe, God, Buddha, Allah, Tony Robbins, Dr. Phil, whoever or whatever—damn it, it's their fault that I am twice-divorced!

The blame game—it should be destroyed along with paparazzi, critics and all the people behind the homogenization of America with all the Super WalMart/Mas Grande Target/Lowes/ Bed Bath & Beyond/Old Navy/Best Buy shopping centers in every freaking city in America. Don't get me started! Oh, I forgot to add lawyers to that list.

We put way too much responsibility on "Destiny," "Fate," "God," and the "Universe." Think about it. It's a helluva a lot easier to blame the state of our lives on some mysterious unseen third party who can't speak. They would probably say, "No, you dumb ass—it's not my fault, it's yours."

I look again to gain some spiritual enlightenment from my dear beloved friend, Pooh. I am going to quote the whole section because it is so important to me.

"In order to take control of our lives and accomplish something of lasting value, sooner or later we need to learn to Believe. We don't need to shift our responsibilities onto the shoulders of some deified Spiritual Superman, or sit around and wait for Fate to come knocking at the door. We need to simply believe in the power that's within us, and use it. When we do that, and stop imitating others and competing against them, things begin to work for us." *The Tao of Pooh*—B. Hoff, pg. 120.

I am just sharing a little bit of what I have learned over my two-year journey. It works for me. This is not some hippie diatribe or some new age bullshit. This is about Accepting Responsibility for You.

For the past thirty some odd years, I thought life was 90% destiny and 10% free will. Now, the proponents of this paradigm are as follows:

- If I am not good at something, it just wasn't meant to be.
- If I didn't work hard at something and I failed, it just wasn't meant to be.
- If I lost my job and didn't pound the pavement to get back in the saddle, it is okay because God will take care of me.
- If I royally screwed someone over or hurt someone, it is okay because I am saved and God will forgive me.
- If I make bad decisions, oh well, this is the path that I am supposed to be on.
- If my life sucks and doesn't ever seem to get any better because I don't bother to accept sole responsibility for my life—well, this is the life I was destined to have.
- If I want to change my horrible life circumstances, I will pray about it and if nothing happens then it wasn't meant for me.
- I am a victim and a slave to this mysterious Destiny, Fate, God, Allah, or whoever else's shoulders we choose to lay our misery and our control on.

Frankly, by me placing the blame on Destiny, it made my role in my life a lot easier. It is so much easier to blame Destiny than to actually have to say the following:

"I made a bad decision."

"I am sorry that I am a shit and treated you like crap because I was selfish."

"I am sorry that I broke your heart because I was such a pathetic weakling that I could not just tell you the truth."

"I am sorry that I ran away and hid from everything because I was embarrassed by the poor decisions and bad judgment calls I have made for the past 20+ years."

"I am sorry that I had absolutely no self-control and slept with what's-his-name and caused you pain."

"I am sorry that I am a selfish, self-centered, egotistical bastard of a person who didn't give a damn about your feelings or treat you with the respect that you, at a minimum as another human being who walks this earth with me, deserves to be given."

"I am sorry for all the pain I have ever put upon you all because I couldn't say I was wrong."

Okay, here was what caused the shift of the paradigm—an article written by a guy on death row, written a few days prior to his execution. The gist was this: he did what he did, he screwed up royally in life, and yes, he found God while in prison. HOWEVER, he took full responsibility for his life and accepted his sentence of death. You will have to trust me on this because I didn't have the foresight to keep the life-changing article.

He wrote something to the effect that too many times in life, people put the responsibility of their lives on God or Destiny but the fact of the matter is (in his opinion) God tosses you out here, and after that you are responsible for everything else in life. You make the choices, you do the actions and you are in control of you.

So it didn't matter that he "found God." He still killed someone and he needed to be responsible for his actions. He could blame the state of his life on Destiny, Karma, God, Fate, the universe, whatever—but he didn't.

That right there, my friend, is profound. I didn't get a chance to let this guy know that he had changed my life. He really did. See, he didn't sit there and cry about how hard his life had been or bemoan the cards he had been dealt.

He didn't play the victim of society's ills. You know, the bad neighborhood, drugs, alcohol, welfare, poverty…there were no mysterious evil outside forces that drove him to murder. He could have chosen not to pull the trigger. But he didn't. A law was broken; he admitted his guilt, and yes he was remorseful, but that didn't matter. He walked straight to the gas chamber with the knowledge of…

Profound Insight #3:

Could've, Would've, Should've, But Didn't (and it is no one else's fault but mine). Life is 99% my responsibility and 1% Chance, Destiny, Fate, God or whoever.

"Well, it must be Fate that I will spend my life alone." "Well, when the Universe is ready for me to be in a relationship, it will send me Mr. Right." "Destiny will bring me a loving, happy relationship when I am ready for it."

Destiny & Fate are sitting somewhere saying, "Wasn't me." God is sitting there saying, "Well, let's see, I did send you two relationships. You did a fine job of screwing those up on your own."

The cold hard truth is that unless I want something different in my life, I gotta change me, my thoughts and my actions. Which is of course…

Profound Insight #4:

Accept it, Change it or Leave it—but shut the hell up and stop bitching about it.

Now, that may sound a little harsh. But see, I am very impatient. Yes, I am always go, go, go (at least when I am on an up cycle). It drives me nuts when people whine, moan, groan and overall just bitch about the state of their life but do nothing about it.

I am big on action. I embrace change. Even when it is hard and it hurts. I realized I had to change. I had to accept responsibility for myself and my actions and then do the hard work to become the person I wanted to become.

The old Judy, she wasn't working anymore. I had to first define who I wanted to be. Who is Judy? What does Judy like? What does Judy not like? What are Judy's values? What the hell does Judy really want out of life?

Music is a big part of Judy and it was time to embrace the music. Music is me and I am the music. Music is as much me as my highlighted blonde hair, my black and white pony cowboy boots that I have owned since 1994 and my frequent use of flavorful language sometimes doused with a few f-bombs. Music is as much a part of me as my loud, overdramatic exclamations when hearing unbelievable news: "SHUT UP" or "NO WAY"! These little trademarks, branding logos— they are signature marks of Judy.

I have denied myself music for too long. I sacrificed my love for music for two marriages.

Both husbands hated country music. Country music became my guilty little pleasure that could only be indulged in the privacy of my automobile.

With the freedom of singledom I can sing loudly in my car, my house and yes, I can two-step to George Strait in my own living room. I proclaim in my profile on www.match.com that I am a country music lover and this is one area that cannot be compromised. Music is an integral part of my life and it cannot be denied any longer. It must be nurtured, treasured and cherished.

My profile has a catchy headline that reads, "Wanna get a little mud on the tires?" Well, if a man doesn't know that is a Brad Paisley song, it will clearly show and I must screen him out. If a man's profile says he hates country music, I pass him by.

To some, it may seem like my love for country music is a little thing, something that could be overcome in a relationship. No, no, no it cannot. Opposites do not work on the spectrum of musical love in my life.

You know how I mentioned before that when I was in high school, I had that dream of wearing some hot guy's football jacket? Well, I have another dream. It is a little dream, but it holds a large part of my heart.

My dream is that I am at a Kenny Chesney concert. I am standing with my friends, we are all singing along and good times abound. My blonde hair is blowing in the wind and the smell of fresh cut grass fills the warm August sky. The gentle wind caresses my skin and a song comes on. Not just any song, but my song. The song that tells the world I am his woman. I have it all. I have all the qualities from A-Z. I am the perfect girl. I have all his heart, his soul, his wishes. All of his love, his hugs and his kisses. Yes, I have it all. I got it all.

Is my dream that Kenny is singing directly to me, about me? Well, while that would be great on so many levels, it is highly unlikely. No, no, my dream is that I am standing there singing along with the crowd to "She's Got It All," and there is a guy behind me. His arms are wrapped around my waist and he is singing in my ear to me, because to him, I got it all. He loves me, I love him and we both love music.

That's my dream.

CHAPTER 11
LIFE AIN'T ALWAYS BEAUTIFUL—GARY ALLAN

Before this journey, I feared that I would never find my "soul mate." But now I don't even know if I really even believe in that anymore. I don't know. I mean, I want to believe in it. But it just seems that there are so many shades of love.

I don't know if I buy into this idea that there is only one great love in our lives. I think we love each person differently and sometimes love just isn't enough to make a relationship work.

I think that love is as plentiful in life as songs about love. However, I think that commitment is a rarity. Love is like that one song that takes you to the top of the charts. But love alone— that is just a one-hit wonder. Commitment is what makes a lasting career. Commitment is making hits year after year. Sometimes it's taking some time off, sometimes going through a tough time, sometimes being on top of the charts and sometimes not even cracking the top 50; but commitment has staying power.

One of the main reasons that I love country music is commitment. Commitment of the artists and commitment of the fans. Commitment.

Kenny Rogers is 67 and he has a top ten single out again. Dolly Parton has a new number one hit. Loretta Lynn and Jack White? What a combination—but damn if "Portland, Oregon" isn't an amazing bit of musical art.

Newcomers are welcomed with open arms by country music fans. Josh Gracin didn't make the top three on American Idol, but he is kicking it on the country charts. Gretchen Wilson could kick the asses of Lindsay Lohan, Hillary Duff, and Ashlee and Jessica Simpson all combined. For that matter, Gretchen Wilson should kick their asses—they are wasting musical airwaves.

Country music is a family. A strong, enduring, committed family. We would never allow Kevin Federline to marry into our family. We are pissed at Renee Zellweger for "annulling" a marriage to one of our own. Who the hell annuls a marriage anyway? You cannot annul a marriage. It happened. Divorce is one thing, but annulment? No way.

Yes, we are a strong family. Sometimes, as most families do, we fight amongst ourselves. Toby Keith and the Dixie Chicks—I'm talking to you guys—it's time to make up. It is time for the Chicks to get back on the road. SheDaisy, while sweet and cute, are no Chicks—so c'mon. Everybody kiss and make up.

It is one big, beautiful family that I love and am glad to be a part of. Hell yeah!

Family, love and commitment. Three things I was not very good at it. I had distanced myself from my own family for quite a while. Living in another state allowed me to have a nice big buffer.

In 2004, I reconnected with my three cousins that I grew up with. My dad is from Ohio and my family would spend time every summer there on the farm. Growing up, I had been very close to my cousins. Keep in mind that my sister is 12 years older than me and my brother is 10 years older than me so I felt like an only child for the most part.

Val is three years older than me, Jeanie is one year younger than me and Joanie is three years younger than me. We reconnected for a weekend, a spur of the moment thing. I had not been to Ohio since I was 17. I briefly had seen the girls at a wedding or funeral once or twice over the past 20 years.

It absolutely was one the best times in my life. I had felt all my life as if I was alone, adrift in a huge vast ocean, just a little tiny head bobbing in the water trying to stay afloat. That weekend, it felt like home. It was as if we had never been apart. The connection, the acceptance and the unconditional love were overwhelming. My relationship with the three of them filled the void.

It is a relationship that I nurture, treasure and cherish. We all email daily and see each other often. The relationship that I have with each of my sister/cousins (that's what I call them because the word cousin doesn't do it justice) is different from the other but just as special. Just as my relationship with my own sister and my best friend is special it is different from my relationship with Val, Jean and Joan.

Love comes in many shades and all are just as beautiful as the other.

When I first started therapy back in December 2003, I felt lost, empty and hopeless. I cried nonstop. I sat in a stupor with my eyes dull and glazed over.

Dr. Alexander would pester me over and over and ask, "What is it you are so afraid of?" I'm afraid of being alone. She would ask "And what is so wrong with that?"

It took lots of hours in therapy first with Dr. Alexander and then Tom Watkins to get to the root of all my problems. I had to learn to parent myself. I had to learn to give myself the unconditional love and nurturing that I deserve and ultimately, Grow Up. I was 35 but mentally and emotionally, I was still that rebellious, bull-headed, egotistical 17-year-old from Tampa.

I am a good person. Most people are good people. I have just made some very bad judgment calls over the past twenty years. I am a good person but I have made some bad decisions. I am not my bad decisions. I did the best I could with the skills that I had at that time in life. I look at myself in the mirror and I say out loud, "I am a good person who has made some bad decisions."

Here I am now at the end of this long journey. I've been alone for two years now, alone and content, alone and at peace with being alone, alone but not lonely.

I dream of a big family. I dream of a husband and a couple of kids. I dream of making new family traditions. We all go to the Kenny Chesney concerts in Raleigh. My little one will wear a shirt that says, "I think his tractor's sexy." We sit around the bonfire at Joan's house in Ohio every memorial day, talking while roasting marshmallows. We go to Country Concert in Ohio every July in Jean and Jay's RV. Every November we celebrate my birthday in St. John; we stay for a whole month and play in Maho Bay. Every Christmas Eve we watch "Holiday Inn" with Bing Crosby and sing along to "White Christmas."

I look around and I do see happy, successful married couples around me. I have a list of couples that do the hard work and put in the time and energy to maintain their relationship. It is clear to me that both parties love and respect each other. They are committed to making it work, no matter what. They are comfortable within their own selves to be comfortable in their union.

Yeah, sometimes I do get sad and have a little pity party for myself. I plug in my iPod, select Rainy Sad Mood Playlist and blast Gary Allan's "Life Ain't Always Beautiful." I mope and pout and say am I ever going to meet this guy? I'm ready now, I have done the hard work, I faced my demons…where is this guy? Is there a guy? I did my 99%, what else can I do?

My friends, Andy and Dick, have been married for 35 years and they are still as cute and in love as a young teenage couple. They have worked long and hard on it. Andy once told me that ultimately it comes down to a lot of hard work and being committed to the marriage. Not just committed to the man, but committed to the family.

Her daughter is embarrassed because of the outgoing message on the family answering machine. I told her to keep it because I love it! It is Andy's voice saying to leave a message because they aren't home and then you can hear Dick making her laugh and they end up giggling and being silly. I love the message because it reminds me of the type of relationship that I want. They laugh together, they play together, and their love shows.

As cheesy as this may sound, another couple on my list is Tim McGraw and Faith Hill. When you watch them in separate interviews and they talk about the other…it is amazing. They adore each other and take care to protect and maintain the family that they have created.

Recently, at Woody's in St. John, I coordinated an impromptu wedding reception for Aimee and Chris Lyon. They had just married on the beach and were celebrating in true Caribbean fashion. I took it upon myself to throw the reception, even though I had just met them. I wanted to make this day everything that it should be. I do know a little something about getting married.

I appointed myself the wedding reception coordinator, maid of honor and best man. The waitresses were the bridesmaids, the guys in the kitchen were the groomsmen, the bar manager was the ring bearer and a patron of the bar was the flower girl.

Holding my glass of sugar-free red bull above my head, kneeling upon a stool in front of the bar, I gave the toast:

"To our dear friends Aimee and Chris, whom we have just met. We are honored that you chose to celebrate your union with us at Woody's. We wish you the best and we wish you the strength and patience to do the hard work. After two weddings and two divorces, I offer you this advice:

Profound Insight #5

Always treat each other as though you are in the first three months of dating. Don't take each other for granted, don't treat each other as if you've known each other for years so it doesn't matter, treat each other with respect and care and be on your best behavior at all times. If you treat each other as if you are in those precious first three months when you are still trying to win each other over by impressing the other with how wonderful and caring you really are—you can't go wrong."

They needed to have their first dance. The lights were dimmed and we all looked on quietly with smiles on our faces. I chose a song for them, "You Save Me," by Kenny Chesney. They danced right there in the middle of that little itty-bitty island bar. Aimee looked gorgeous in her wedding dress and Target sequined flip-flops. Chris, handsome in his suit, gazed into her eyes.

We patrons at the bar that night were allowed to be a part of an incredible little moment of time in two people's lives.

There—that tiny little nanosecond in the big gigantic spectrum of time. That is the statistical anomaly that I mentioned before. It is that one moment in time, where two people are bound together by a moment of intimacy. That is the statistical anomaly that can't be replicated and can't be manufactured. It is a special combination of place, time, atmosphere, a little magic, some chemistry, and a whole helluva of a lot of hard work and it all comes together in a tiny little space between two people. If you look close enough and pay close attention, you really can see love. You can see the color of it, the energy of it and the power of it.

I want to believe that there is a Mr. Long Term Meaningful Committed Relationship That Will Not End in Divorce out there for me. He will view the world in an optimistic way like me, he'll have a zest for life, he will be able to understand the dualistic nature of my artistic/creative side blended with the business acumen of a shark, he will love music (specifically country, damn it), he will value security, adventure, fun, family and love. He will feel like coming home, and as Faith once said about Tim, he will feel like that special favorite old shirt that you sleep in every night.

I want to have the beginning moments of Aimee and Chris and the lasting moments of Andy and Dick, thirty years down the road. I want it all.

I want the Venn Diagram of Relationships. Complimentary, not completion. I don't go for that Jerry McGuire nonsense of "You complete me." I am complete (finally…damn it, took long enough!) I want someone who compliments me. I want the Venn Diagram. You know, that thing from high school. Me in one circle, him in another circle and a family in the third circle—they all overlap, yet they are complete in themselves, independent yet interdependent.

The older you get as a woman, the smaller your pool of possible suitors gets. And that sucks ass. Don't even mention that whole Demi Moore—Ashton Kutcher thing. I don't have the patience or energy to put up with a guy who is 20 years younger than me. Which in my case would be 15, and that is just gross.

I'm not into that. I want a guy who has been through life's experiences, can understand references to movies from the 80s and knows that Pearl Jam came first, not Nirvana. One who knows that Axl Rose actually used to be an amazing rocker, one who does not sit and watch "Pimp My Ride" every day and buy clothes by Sean John, one who knows that Sean John has had way too many names by now, a guy who actually knows that Jennifer Lopez was a fly-girl on In Living Color back in the day before she became so overrated, and one who knows that Mariah Carey is just a woman in her mid-thirties trying to cling onto her 22-year-old self by doing songs with The Neptunes and the Ying Yang Twins.

I want a guy who has been through long-term relationships. Preferably I'd like a guy who has been married before so he knows what it takes to make a relationship work. I want a guy who knows the difference between sex and intimacy. I want a guy who knows who he is and has made his own way, and who is also looking for the Venn Diagram of Relationships.

I am talking about a pool of possible suitors for a Long-Term Committed Meaningful Relationship That Will Not End in Divorce. Not random hook-ups, not casual sex, not dating to date. I can take myself out to eat, I can go to the movies with friends, I can buy my own diamonds, I can take myself on vacations and yes, I can even take care of myself sexually. Plus, I know my body and I know what the hell it takes to have an orgasm. I don't want some young 'un who doesn't know his way around a woman's body. Oh—and I ain't no Mrs. Robinson. Get your own damn teacher.

After having the experience of having sex with someone that I truly loved, I actually saw the statistical anomaly of intimacy in a flash of second, and I knew I couldn't go back to sex without love.

It's lonely. It is physically exhilarating, it is lust, hot heavy sweat-dripping bodies writhing in motion animalistic hunger ravaging each other and climaxing with dual savagery. But then—it is over. Over. Nothing more. Over.

The connection breaks and the bodies separate. They go their own way. Was there really even a connection to begin with? Maybe not. Maybe it was just the raging heat generated between my legs. Now it is over. My lust is quenched and nothing remains.

Me and the man with whom I just bared my body, my innermost animal instincts, we will go our separate ways. He doesn't really connect with me and I don't connect with him. It's quietly lingering in the room. The gentle lingering of why.

Why did we just do that? Did we both want the same thing? Was it just a physical urge? Why am I really hiding my real thoughts? Do I really believe that sex can just be sex? Why do you not like me like I like you? Why don't you love me? Why? Will I see you tomorrow? Will you just pull a Heisman and never talk to me again? Will I now look at you and grimace inside because you left me hanging but got the orgasm you so desperately needed? Will I roll over and think that I may be falling in love with you? Will I think to myself how, how do I tell him that I don't feel the same way?

Why? Why does sex have to be so emotionally exhausting for me? Why? Why would I rather just be alone, with headphones on, eyes closed, lounging in the comfort and security of my musical cocoon?

Why? Because I feel a connection. A connection to the music and I don't feel so alone. Because regardless of my complete irrelevance to Kenny Chesney the living breathing man, I know that there is one other person on this planet who is just like me. We think alike, we have similar dreams, we love the islands and we share the same voice. I am not alone. I have found a kindred spirit on this vast planet. That is enough for me.

Recently, I was on an 11-hour international flight. After a couple of hours of reading and roaming the aisle, I stretched my legs in bulkhead and eyed my backpack. It was time. It is time to pull out the iPod and zone out. I had carefully guarded the battery level. I needed to have enough to get home. I had been without music for over a week.

Closing my eyes, I kicked back and scrolled the menu. What did I need to hear? What would soothe my soul? I had skipped over my Chesney playlist; I was getting to be a bit Chesney'ed out after the book and all. I played a few songs but just couldn't seem to find the right thing. I was fidgety; I couldn't seem to settle in.

Finally, I took a deep sigh of reluctant acceptance and rolled my eyes. Why even fight it? The fact of the matter is that he is my old reliable. That damn Chesney voice wraps over my soul like the old pinwheel quilt my grandmother made me. It is warm, soothing, comforting and just plain ol' familiar. Snuggled into my delta blankie, I closed my eyes and the music flowed over me.

Things can change, life can move fast, life can move slow, and sometimes life stops. But no matter my age, my geographic location, my weight, my hairstyle, or my marital status, the music stays the same. It is my old blue chair. As I sat in 22c, Delta #47 somewhere over the Atlantic Ocean, I thought about the changes in life that were coming my way. I thought about how far I have come emotionally, spiritually, and mentally and I looked forward with a sense of peace. And I can now look back with a sense of peace.

I am in a state of peace. Just be. Sit in the blue chair and just be. "In This Boat Alone" appeared on my iPod. It is a bonus track on Chesney's *The Road and the Radio* CD. I think about my own boat. It took me a long time to be able to own my boat. I fought long and hard against myself to be the Captain. I have been for some time. I have had lots of guests in and out of my boat. Some great adventures, some not so great, but I have become pretty good at navigating the rough waters.

I have come to realize lately that it would be nice to have someone else at the helm for a while. Someone else steering the boat, with me hanging onto him. I think maybe, with the right person, I could be content with being first mate. I have a hard time letting go of my independence. But I think, with the right man, I'd let him Captain the boat for a while. The right man, this Mr. LTCMRTWNEID, he'll be strong enough to let me take the wheel when I want to. Because I think marriage isn't really a true partnership, it isn't always equal and it isn't always fifty-fifty. Just like the tides ebb and flow, so does a marriage. I recognize this and I'm ready to stay in the boat for the whole voyage.

With the music filling my brain, I drifted back to thoughts of St. John. It had been several months since my visit but Chesney's music pulled me back. I was sitting on the ferry dock waiting for the next boat to St. Thomas and I met a spectacular man. Seriously magnificent. A pure, genuine, authentic, lovely soul.

His name is Alexander. He is probably in his late 70's. He is a tall thin St. Johnian, and he has lived on the island all of his years. He was on his way to St. Thomas for his bi-weekly kidney analysis. I was lying on a bench with my backpack as my pillow, eyes closed and iPod cranked up. He sat beside me and the next thing I knew I was engrossed in a warm conversation with this lovely gentleman.

I caught him looking at my left hand and I laughed aloud. He said in his aged Caribbean accent, "Well, I see no ring. How is it that a beautiful girl is not taken?" I said smiling, "Because I have two rings in a box at home." He smiled, looked away and then looked me in the eye and very slowly said, "Hmm...well then, you either do not make good decisions or you are too picky."

Looking into his faded yet still twinkling warm caramel eyes, I said, "You know what, Alexander? I think I have made some bad decisions and now I'm afraid that I am too picky."

My adventure to St. John was very good for my self-esteem. After an extremely long period of no dates, no flattery and no interest, I was hit on consistently by very good-looking young guys, every night, every hour on the hour.

The attention was quite overwhelming. A little overdue, but definitely overwhelming! But I'm not an idiot. At least, not anymore.

I now know the difference between being wanted and being loved. I get tired of being the "prize" to be won. I get tired of the bullshit that guys say to "win the prize" of getting a piece of Judy ass. I get tired of the Smile and Nod while some drunk rambles on incoherently about how beautiful I am, how sexy I am, curvy, smart, blah, blah, blah. Same bullshit, different day, different guy—same waste of my energy.

Yes, it is nice to meet new people. But honestly, my circle of friends is big enough. My opinion is that most guys want to get into the circle of friends to get into the pants of Judy. And it is soooooo predictable and redundant and spent.

I've done the online dating thing; I have gotten tons of emails from probably very nice guys. I have gone on dates with very nice, upstanding guys. I have dated a couple of guys that I really liked for several months…but they weren't Mr. Long Term Meaningful Committed Relationship That Will Not End in Divorce.

I am so done with it and I am so exhausted by it.

Surprisingly to myself, I now can clearly see the bullshit that guys hand me. The low self-esteem that drove me to jump every guy that looked my way in my previous life is gone. That Judy was put to rest.

I performed a ritual. I needed to let go. Cinnamon Bay was the site chosen for my burial at sea. The old Judy served me well. She was so many things, but it was time to put her down. She had lived a long, hard life for 35 years. On December 1, 2005 at 5:45 p.m. the eulogy was given and the ashes of Judy Core were sprinkled into the sea.

Among those ashes were ashes of old boyfriends, negative critical self-image thoughts, names of those I'd rather forget, events that I can't really remember, bad habits, and all the emotional negative energy that had ultimately killed her. So with a few tears and kind words, the needy and clingy girl begging to be loved, the emotionally high-maintenance, crying at the drop of the hat, hyper-sensitive, out of control, drunk party girl was set free.

The circle of life—she was freed so that a birth could occur.

This was the birth of the confident, strong, emotionally stable, sober, funny, sweet, loving, nurturing woman who was filled with inner peace and calm. She is a responsible adult who cherishes her magical child-likeness and understands that it is a wonderful part of her.

She appreciates the focus and drive that have made her a partner in a real estate development company, the chief operating officer of several companies, a dedicated life-long learner who wants to make a difference in the lives around her, and whose passion is female adolescent development. She is a strong mentor and a patient listener. She relates well and speaks openly and honestly with the teenage girls whom she mentors.

She still loves deeply and passionately, but she is wise in her use of boundaries and knows how to protect her heart and soul without using anger as a wall.

She is a woman who knows that dreams are just goals that you aren't fully committed to yet. She understands the need for priorities and adaptability. She doesn't just wish it: if it is that important, she just does it.

She knows that you can't change people and that we all learn our lessons in due time. She is more patient and loving to those around her. She understands the importance of fun and play on a daily basis!

She is one who will be a good, loving mother to her future children, a loyal, supporting, devoted, committed wife to her future husband and a woman who possesses the emotional inner strength needed to weather any storm that life may bring. She is someone who this author is proud to associate with, and she is my best friend. Personally, this author holds her in the highest regard and thinks she is the bombdiggity.

Judy M. Core was born there on the shores of Cinnamon Bay. And she is spectacular.

CHAPTER 12
AMAZING—ALEX LLOYD

So now that I have made all this meaningful progress and deemed my journey of self-destruction to self-evolution a success, what do I do now?

Let's review to see what is still on the To Do List to Fix Judy. Been sober for almost two years—Check Good job! Stayed on medication and got off emotional roller coaster—Check. Stayed in therapy and dealt with self esteem—Check, self esteem is in good working order. Stayed in therapy to resolve boundary issues with men, parenting the self and dissolve all previously held myths about relationships and marriage—Check, done good! Learn what commitment means—Check, I have a full working definition and plan to use it. Defined the qualities of Mr. Long Term Meaningful Committed Relationship That Will Not End in Divorce in order to recognize him in case I should run into him on the street—Check, all in order, but I would like to mention that if he, Mr. LTMCRTWNEID, just happened to be Chris Cagle, that would be okay too. I would not have a problem with that at all.

Well alrighty then, hmmm…what to do now. Write a book? Sounds like a pretty good idea. I think that I have made a pretty strong case for why good music is better than sex. Some may agree, some may disagree, but to each his own. I hope that everyone at some point in their life is able to find something that they are passionate about.

I hope that people who need a voice will find a voice. Maybe they won't find their voice in Kenny Chesney, but maybe they will find their voice somewhere. Maybe, just maybe, someone will find his or her voice with me.

Then maybe one day someone somewhere will experience a moment of pure bliss and then smile and say quietly to his or herself, "That is some good shit. That is better than sex."

So what do you think? Do I sit around twiddling my thumbs waiting for Mr. LTMCRTWNEID? Do I sit around and dream about him? Should I pray for hours on end? Should I try to increase my good karma so that maybe good things will come my way?

Good God no.

Did you not pay attention to the whole thing about the 99% rule of Responsibility? It is time to come to grips with living this life as if this mythical magical man who will share my life and my love will actually not ever arrive.

There is a Buddhist saying: Abandon Hope. Hmm, what the hell does that mean?

Hope is what keeps us going, keeps us alive right? It keeps us always keeping on, so to speak. When I first heard this, I thought this was the most foreign concept and worst advice I had ever heard.

Abandon Hope? It makes me speechless, without speech, befuddled, confused. Why would we abandon hope? What would there be to live for?

Well, here is the thing with this little Buddhist gem of wisdom: Hope keeps us wanting more. It keeps us desiring more stuff. Stuff like more shoes, more house, more money, more clothes, more love, more, more, more. It never ends.

More. More. More. When is enough, actually enough? Will more stuff make us more happy?

Is happiness a destination? Is it some magical, mythical place where we arrive and the golden gates open widely to allow us in? In this magical land of Happiness, do rainbows appear, do fairies flit about and birds sing "Moon River" by Andy Williams?

Do we all of a sudden appear more beautiful, more physically fit? Are all those little things we hate about ourselves magically gone? Does a chime sound majestically throughout the Hills of Happiness land and do all of our troubles disappear, credit cards magically paid off, student loans forgiven and…does the perfect ideal man appear next to us in bed?

No. No, this doesn't happen, does it? But aren't we always saying we will be Happy when…? I will be happy when my house is sold. I will be happy when I meet so and so, I will be happy when I lose ten pounds. I will be happy when I get a boob job. I will be Happy…when?

Abandon Hope. I thought long and hard about this. What would happen if I abandoned all hope, all my desires, my dreams, and my wishes?

If I gave up all of that, I would live as if today was my last. I would live in the moment. I would be in the moment. I would stop wishing and dreaming and be. I would just be.

I would look at everything around me. I would be still. I would be satisfied with everything around me. Why? Because I wouldn't know of anything else.

There would be no anticipation, no wanting. There would not be a constant state of "wanting-ness." Wanting-ness is bad.

Eeyore once said that when it comes to enjoying life and making use of who we are, we can't. Eeyore. You know, that pain in the butt, pessimistic critic Eeyore, the party of life buzz-kill.

When you follow the Way of Pooh, you just ignore Eeyore because you know differently, you know that it isn't because we can't—it is because we don't. We are content with our jar of honey. We are content to be that simple-minded little bear named Pooh.

That guy who wrote the *Tao of Pooh* is a genius. He tells us that it is, in Pooh-speak, attributable to the Tiddely Pom Principle. You know, it in other words… maybe the snowball effect, the downward spiral of negativeness, the tsunami of cynicism. It is so easy to get caught up in the downward spiral.

However, it is extremely hard to get people caught up in the upward spiral.

So if I Abandon Hope, if I say Happiness is NOT a destination, if I stop and just be, for one second, one moment. No speaking, no thinking, no acting, just being.

I see that It was there all along. It…who is it, what is it? It is happiness, fulfillment, contentment, peace, and calm.

There is that dang blue chair again. If I just sit still for one moment and just be, I will hear the beautiful stillness of the music of my life. I am sitting in the blue chair. I am safe.

Following the Way of Pooh, sitting in my blue chair, and ensuring that my head, heart and heated loins were in alignment, I recently made a Decision. A Very Big Decision, as Pooh would say.

This decision had been pondered for several years, with lots of research and lots of preparedness.

All these life lessons that I have shared with my dear readers over the past many pages were faced head-on for one reason and one reason only.

I want to be a good mother. I knew that I needed to Grow Up and put all this crap behind me so that I could be a good mother. And I will be a good mother. I know I will. I am ready.

While it would be nice to have Mr. Long Term Meaningful Committed Relationship That Will Not End in Divorce in my life prior to making this decision, I am choosing to not wait.

The Eeyores of the world have let me know their opinions, as have Rabbit, Owl and Piglet. They have all let me know their concerns, their issues and their political positions. But Kanga, friend of Pooh and mother to Roo, she understands. She knows.

Currently, I am in the process of adopting a little girl from Russia. My dossier has been sent to Russia and I have done my 99%. Now that 1% is in God's hands. At the end of the process, I know in my heart that I will hold the little one that is meant to be my child.

It was not a decision to be made lightly. But it is the right decision for me.

What about candidates for Mr. Long Term Meaningful Committed Relationship That Will Not End in Divorce?

There will be a very intensive screening process for this man. It has to be this way because not every man can be a daddy to my child. A daddy is someone very special. He must meet a lot of very strict requirements.

I will have to be very picky if and when I finally choose him. I am choosing for two now and I am playing for keeps. We won't be actively looking, but if we stumble upon him, we will know it. Head, heart and heated loins will be in alignment.

He'll take the wheel of the ship and he'll have some itty bitty life jackets for my little one. He will be the one who is able to sit in the blue chair with us, listening to our music and creating new life soundtracks with us. He will follow the Way of Pooh with us and will readily sign the required legal partnership documents that will make him officially Mr. Long Term Meaningful Committed Relationship That Will Not End in Divorce.

Then he will put the pen down and we will just be.